Easy to Read
LARGE PRINT

Too Blessed
to be Stressed

3-MINUTE DEVOTIONS
FOR WOMEN

Too Blessed to be Stressed

3-MINUTE DEVOTIONS FOR WOMEN

Debora M. Coty

BARBOUR BOOKS

An Imprint of Barbour Publishing, Inc.

ISBN 978-1-64352-268-5

Compiled by JoAnne Simmons.

Published in association with the literary agency of WordServe Literary Group, Ltd., www.word-serveliterary.com.

Published by Barbour Books, an imprint of Barbour Publishing, Inc., 1810 Barbour Drive, Uhrichsville, Ohio 44683, www.barbourbooks.com.

Our mission is to inspire the world with the life-changing message of the Bible.

Printed in the United States of America.

GOT 3 MINUTES TO SPARE?

You'll find just the spiritual pick-me-up you need in *Too Blessed to be Stressed: 3-Minute Devotions for Women.* These 180 uplifting readings from bestselling author Debora M. Coty pack a powerful dose of comfort, encouragement, humor, and inspiration into your day.

Minute 1: scripture to meditate on
Minute 2: a short devotional reading
Minute 3: a prayer to jump-start a conversation with God

Read on. . .and be blessed!

PAPA GOD

*To all who did receive him, to those who
believed in his name, he gave the
right to become children of God.*

JOHN 1:12 NIV

I'm often asked why I refer to God as "Papa God."
The reason is simple: because He is. My Papa. Your
Papa. When we make the decision to believe in Him,
to receive the unconditional love demonstrated by the
sacrifice of His only Son, Jesus, in our place, we're
adopted into Papa's family. We become His beloved,
adored, cherished daughters. Hey, we might not think
we're much, but He thinks we're to die for!

The intimate term in the Bible for *God the Father* is
the Aramaic word *Abba,* the name Jesus referred to
Him by and offered to share with us as Papa's adopted
children (Romans 8:15). Children specifically chosen.
Handpicked. *Wanted. The Message* translates *Abba*
as "Papa." I totally love that. It's warm, protective, and
delightfully cuddly. What name could more richly express
our close relationship with our heavenly Daddy?

. . . .

*Dear Papa God, You are my heavenly Daddy,
a good and gracious Papa. Thank You for wanting
me and loving me enough to die for me. Amen.*

LIGHT AND BEAUTY

"Are you tired? Worn out? Burned out on religion? Come to me. Get away with me and you'll recover your life. I'll show you how to take a real rest."
MATTHEW 11:28 MSG

God desires only to colorize our black-and-white world and refill it with light and beauty. "'Keep company with me and you'll learn to live freely and lightly'" (Matthew 11:30 MSG). We have to be willing to sneak up on ourselves and rest in an unexpected beautiful moment before we can talk ourselves out of it through reason and sensibility, schedules and agendas.

Living life, after all, is a series of conscious decisions, an act of the will. So it's up to us to choose to slow down enough to enjoy snapshots of beauty—like impromptu violin concerts, spiderwebs, sunbeams, and puppies—that bring rest and peace to our weary souls.

. . . .

Dear Papa God, please allow me to rock, rest, and revive in Your loving embrace today. Thank You, Father, that no matter what comes my way, You will give me rest on every side (1 Kings 5:4 NIV). Amen.

FEAR CAN BE A GOOD THING

"Don't panic. I'm with you. There's no need to fear
for I'm your God. I'll give you strength. I'll help you.
I'll hold you steady, keep a firm grip on you."
ISAIAH 41:10 MSG

Papa God gave us the emotion of fear for good reason. It serves a useful purpose—to motivate us, move us forward, and keep us from making mistakes. Sometimes fear saves us from ourselves. Why else would we faithfully squash our bosom buddies flat with mammograms unless there were the possibility of that frightening C word invading our bodies? We could be out pounding the pavement if fear of losing our jobs didn't motivate us to get our reports in on time.

It's when fear becomes controlling that it debilitates. When it alters our course from the splendid women Papa God intended us to be and makes us settle for a wimpy, whiny imitation. Or when it begins to dictate our thoughts and behavior.

. . . .

Dear Papa God, please help me to have a
healthy attitude about fear. Let it spur me to
action when needed, and let it always prompt
me to pray and draw closer to You. Amen.

A VIBRANT LIFE FORCE

The Spirit of God, who raised Jesus from the dead, lives in you. And just as God raised Christ Jesus from the dead, he will give life to your mortal bodies by this same Spirit living within you.

ROMANS 8:11 NLT

Vultures aren't intimidated by lifeless carrion, but pit them against a vibrant life force and they're overwhelmed.

That's how we get rid of our spiritual vultures too—we seek help from the biggest, most powerful life force there is. Those unseen carnivores bringing us down can't remain in His presence.

"The Spirit who lives in you is greater than the spirit who lives in the world" (1 John 4:4 NLT). That, dear sister, is the difference between an unholy spirit and the Holy Spirit. One has a BB gun and the other has a bazooka. And the enforcer's on our side.

Spiritual warfare in a nutshell.

. . . .

Dear Papa God, please help me to have confidence in and seek help constantly from Your all-powerful Spirit that You've given me. Amen.

DEAL WITH IT

Go ahead and be angry. You do well to be angry—but don't use your anger as fuel for revenge. And don't stay angry. . . . Don't give the Devil that kind of foothold in your life.
EPHESIANS 4:26–27 MSG

As hard it as might be, you must deal with your anger. Acknowledge that it's there, even if it's buried deep beneath layers of denial. But maybe you think it's not "Christian" to be indignant or you've become proficient at stuffing your animosity. Listen, girlfriend, if you've been rejected and just can't seem to get over it, anger is most likely at the root of your festering wound. It's time to heal that nasty thing so that you're no longer afraid of feeling vulnerable and exposed. Remember, it's not a sin to feel mad. Injustice is *supposed* to make Christ-followers bristle into action. But anger can evolve into resentment, bitterness, or destructive rage if you don't defuse it. And that, most definitely, is sin.

• •

Dear Papa God, I need to deal with this anger I have, and I need Your help. Please let me give it to You—again and again if need be— and thank You for taking it. Amen.

FEARFULLY AND WONDERFULLY MADE

I will give thanks to You, for I am fearfully and wonderfully made; wonderful are Your works, and my soul knows it very well.

PSALM 139:14 NASB

Do you accept yourself for who you are? Recognize that you are not defined by what you do, but by whom Papa God ultimately designed you to be. And remember, you're a work still in progress. Your actions do *not* dictate who you are and whether or not you're acceptable to Him. You are! My friend Philip said it well: "Your self-esteem is not derived from your performance or how nice your car, or house, or even how your body looks. Your self-worth comes from the One who created you, and He's already shown you what He thinks of you by sending His beloved only Son to die in your place." *That's* how important you are, dear sister.

. . . .

Dear Papa God, it's so easy to be unhappy with myself. Help me to embrace that You've made me fearfully and wonderfully unique, and You love me more than I can comprehend. Amen.

WORRY WON'T HELP

"Who of you by worrying can add a single hour to your life? Since you cannot do this very little thing, why do you worry about the rest?"

L<small>UKE</small> 12:25–26 <small>NIV</small>

Do you tend to blow things out of proportion? People with a history of rejection tend to read more rejection between the lines of simple, innocent, everyday transactions. Your friend is *not* abandoning you just because she's too busy to go with you to the concert. Your boss very likely isn't about to fire you simply because he asked you to proofread your report. Okay, take a deep breath. Now exhale. Acknowledge that Papa God is in control and that your petty worrying will not change a single thing. Overinflating every balloon into a spy dirigible will only make *you* explode.

. . . .

Dear Papa God, I tend to overanalyze and give myself anxiety over nothing. Please help me to direct my worrisome thoughts to You and exchange them for Your peace. Amen.

LOVED AND ADORED

You watched me as I was being formed in utter seclusion, as I was woven together in the dark of the womb. . . . How precious are your thoughts about me, O God. They cannot be numbered! I can't even count them; they outnumber the grains of sand! And when I wake up, you are still with me!
PSALM 139:15, 17–18 NLT

Do you understand how valuable you are? Cherished. Loved without limits. *Wanted.* At this moment, you may feel abandoned, or forsaken, or betrayed, but feelings are not trustworthy and can change at the drop of a rogue hormone. Now is the time to overrule your heart with your head. Reread that scripture above. See how intimately your Papa God knows and adores you? You've gotta love that last line! He's *still* with you even though He knows you better than anyone in the entire world: inside out, failures and successes, rotten habits, and weird quirks. He will never leave you. He's absolutely dedicated to you!

. . . .

Dear Papa God, thank You for loving me so well, so unconditionally. Forgive me when I forget Your love, and help me to love and cherish You. Amen.

HIS HANDIWORK

*For we are God's handiwork, created in
Christ Jesus to do good works, which
God prepared in advance for us to do.*
EPHESIANS 2:10 NIV

Does your self-esteem need a boost? Sure, everybody has weaknesses, but everybody has strengths too. Find out what your strengths and talents are; assess your spiritual gifts and dominant personality traits (Google "personality tests"—there are tons of choices). Ask your pastor, spouse, or a trusted friend to review the results with you and identify your strengths. Now focus your energies for service in these areas; set yourself up for success. When you find your niche, you'll feel great about yourself, and you'll also feel Papa God's warm, encouraging smile.

. . . .

*Dear Papa God, I want to do Your will with the
unique strengths and gifts You've given me.
Please help me to bring glory to You. Amen.*

CHUCK THE CHUMPS AND GO FOR IT

Forgetting what is behind and straining toward what is ahead, I press on toward the goal to win the prize for which God has called me heavenward in Christ Jesus.
PHILIPPIANS 3:13–14 NIV

Past failure doesn't dictate future failure. Ever hear "You can't do that; it's impossible"? This world is full of those who discourage rather than encourage. If we listen to them, we'll never do anything. If we truly believe that God has called us for a particular purpose, we'll keep going for it despite our track record. Author Frank Peretti was turned away by dozens of publishers before his faith-charging books *This Present Darkness* and *Piercing the Darkness* took the world by storm and drew tens of thousands to their knees. What if he had stopped trying after the nineteenth rejection? What if you stop after yours?

. . . .

Dear Papa God, please give me wisdom to know and work toward the goals You want for me— and to never give up on them. Amen.

LISTEN TO THE RIGHT VOICE

*If you need wisdom, ask our generous God,
and he will give it to you. He will not rebuke
you for asking. But when you ask him,
be sure that your faith is in God alone.*

JAMES 1:5–6 NLT

We all have those little voices speaking over our shoulders: the wise voice and the stupid voice. The wise voice says, "It's okay to like yourself. After all, God is proud of you—you're one of His faves." The stupid voice counters with, "You're a worthless loser; who could possibly like you?" The wise voice suggests, "Get to know Papa God better through prayer and His Word." The stupid voice says, "Just keep doing what you've been doing; nothing will ever change anyway." The wise voice whispers, "Invest yourself in relationships, not stuff that will only rust and decay; make precious lasting memories with those you love." The stupid voice shouts, "People are too risky. They'll only dump you when they get to know the real you. Buy another flashy car."

So which voice do you choose to listen to?

. . . .

Dear Papa God, I need to hear Your voice loudly and clearly in this fallen world. Please help me to listen to and learn from Your Spirit and Your Word. Amen.

17

WRECKING BALL OF MERCY

There is no condemnation for those who belong to Christ Jesus. And because you belong to him, the power of the life-giving Spirit has freed you from the power of sin that leads to death.

Romans 8:1–2 NLT

What do we do when, after we repent and ask Jesus for a sledgehammer to take a few swings at that dividing wall, guilt continues to plague us? We may respond in shame, anger, or depression, which only serves as mortar to fortify the wall.

Why won't the guilt stop? Because Satan, the archenemy of our souls, is using our guilt to strengthen that despicable wall and separate us from our Lord. He accuses us mercilessly and racks us with guilt that makes us feel worthless and unworthy of Papa God's love.

Listen to me right now: it's a lie.

The Accuser underestimates our Savior's mercy. Yes, mercy: that incredibly powerful, wall-obliterating wrecking ball that is Papa God's specialty.

. . . .

Dear Papa God, please wreck the wall that's between us. I long for Your mercy to shatter my guilt and bring me back close to You after I've failed and repented. Amen.

NO MATTER WHAT WE'VE DONE

If we confess our sins, He is faithful and righteous to forgive us our sins and to cleanse us from all unrighteousness.

1 JOHN 1:9 NASB

No matter what we've done, Papa God can repair, restore, and revitalize the remnants of our lives for His higher glory.

It's true. Believe it. Then act like you believe it.

Look at our biblical examples: Rahab the harlot, David the murderer, Jacob the deceiver, and Peter the betrayer. All made terrible choices that resulted in heinous sin. Yes, they were guilty. Yet they refused to wallow in guilt over their mistakes. Instead, they rose above the guilt-mire and moved forward in forgiveness to accomplish mighty things for God.

And we can too if we only remember that taking action releases guilt; obsessing over the past doesn't.

. . . .

Dear Papa God, thank You that when I confess, You forgive and cleanse from all unrighteousness, no matter what the sin. Please help me to have confidence and peace and move forward in that truth. Amen.

REDEEMED AND REBOOTED

*Praise be to the God and Father of our Lord Jesus
Christ. . . . In him we have redemption through his
blood, the forgiveness of sins, in accordance with the
riches of God's grace that he lavished on us.*
EPHESIANS 1:3, 7–8 NIV

It's important to acknowledge guilt when guilt is
due. But we don't have to dejectedly walk away from
the Accuser with that guilt weighing us down forever.
We can be forgiven, redeemed, and rebooted. We may
be guilty, but we're not incarcerated in a "guilted" cage.
Mercy has unlocked the door.

"Don't you realize that you become the slave of
whatever you choose to obey? You can be a slave to
sin, which leads to death, or you can choose to obey
God, which leads to righteous living" (Romans 6:16 NLT).

I choose to obey God. How about you? Guilt is not
my master. Jehovah is the boss of me.

. . . .

*Dear Papa God, I am redeemed by Your blood.
Thank You! Please help me to throw off the weight
of guilt and live in the power of Your grace. Amen.*

WORTHLESS WORRY

"Can all your worries add a single moment to your life? And if worry can't accomplish a little thing like that, what's the use of worrying over bigger things?"
Luke 12:25–26 NLT

Worry has no redeeming qualities. It never fulfills its promises. Instead, it drains our energy, adds spider-web wrinkles on our foreheads, and makes us woefully weary.

Worry is a type of simmering fear that doesn't seem like fear at all because it masquerades as taking responsibility. We can easily fool ourselves into thinking we're doing the responsible thing by agonizing over dilemmas. By dwelling on our troubles, we think that we'll somehow become enlightened with magical answers that will change inevitable outcomes. Fretting and stewing and fussing seem perfectly normal because we're so used to it.

But over time, worrying inflates our problems to appear huge. Enormous. Insurmountable. Even bigger than Papa God.

. . . .

Dear Papa God, when I struggle with worry, please remind me how big You are and how Your will prevails in every situation. Amen.

SAPPING OUR JOY

Give all your worries and cares to God,
for he cares about you.
1 PETER 5:7 NLT

Worrying is a lack of trust that Papa God can—and will—take care of us. We believe we're protecting ourselves by obsessing over what the future might whack us upside our head with so we won't be taken by surprise. Like good little Girl Scouts, we want to be prepared.

Oftentimes, worry causes us to live in the future instead of the present, looking ahead to anticipate potential problems before they arise. But living in the present—the here and now—is where real life is. Author Leo Buscaglia said, "Worry never robs tomorrow of its sorrow, it only saps today of its joy."

* *

Dear Papa God, I don't want worry to steal my joy
and gratitude for what You've given me in this
moment. Thank You for taking my worries.
I give them to You now. Amen.

RETRAIN YOUR BRAIN

You will keep in perfect peace all who trust in you,
all whose thoughts are fixed on you!
ISAIAH 26:3 NLT

Our bodies and minds were not designed to withstand chronic worry. That's why our stomachs end up with turmoil-gouged ulcers, it's why mental wards flourish, and it's the reason Xanax even exists. An hour of worrying is ten times more exhausting than an hour of work. Proof that worry is not the lifestyle our Creator intends for us: Jesus Himself said as much in Luke 12:26: "'If worry can't accomplish a little thing. . .what's the use of worrying over bigger things?'" (NLT).

But there's good news. Worry is a learned habit. And since it's learned, it can be unlearned.

How? Well, we have to train our brains to react to troubles in a different way. A calmer, healthier way.

. . . .

Dear Papa God, please help me to train my brain in a new way, not with worry but with fixing my thoughts on You so that You can keep me in perfect peace. Amen.

TAKING RISKS

Farmers who wait for perfect weather never plant. If they watch every cloud, they never harvest. Just as you cannot understand the path of the wind or the mystery of a tiny baby growing in its mother's womb, so you cannot understand the activity of God, who does all things. Plant your seed in the morning and keep busy all afternoon, for you don't know if profit will come from one activity or another—or maybe both.

ECCLESIASTES 11:4–6 NLT

Becoming a risk taker is, well. . .risky. Probably because most of us prefer our safe little lives of relentless repetition. They're just so ding-dang comfortable. Why change something that's no muss, no fuss, to risk appearing ridiculous, or incompetent, or just plain wrong?

I'll tell you why: because God intended our lives to be abundant: "I have come that they may have life, and that they may have it more abundantly" (John 10:10 NKJV). And living abundantly includes facing a series of opportunities that requires taking risks.

. . . .

Dear Papa God, I need Your wisdom to know when to take risks and when to be cautious. I want to live the abundant life You've called me to, for Your glory. Amen.

24

FEELINGS ARE NOT TRUTH

"The Helper, the Holy Spirit, whom the Father will send in My name, He will teach you all things, and bring to your remembrance all that I said to you. Peace I leave with you; My peace I give to you; not as the world gives do I give to you. Do not let your heart be troubled, nor let it be fearful."
JOHN 14:26–27 NASB

Many who overcome anxiety are the ones who refuse to believe the lie that feelings dictate truth—the lie that says because we feel fear gripping our arms, compressing our hearts, and wrapping its tentacles around our windpipes, we have no choice but to allow it to lock us in its smothering embrace. Don't you believe it either. . .feelings do not dictate truth. The reality is that truth should dictate feelings. Fear is not a physical "thing." It can't force you to do anything. Fear only exists in the emotional realm, and you are not a slave to your emotions.

. . . .

Dear Papa God, I don't want to be overwhelmed by my emotions. I want to overwhelm my emotions with Your truth and Your peace. Please help me. Amen.

LOVE CONQUERS FEAR

Perfect love drives out fear.
1 JOHN 4:18 NIV

One of mankind's oldest and strongest emotions is fear. Remember how Adam and Eve fearfully hid from God in the Garden of Eden after they'd sinned? Yep, fear has been around a long time. But we have one very important consolation: the only emotion older and stronger is love. God loved Adam and Eve before and after they'd sinned. Sure, He was disappointed and upset with them because of their disobedience (just like we are when our children disobey us). But He still loved them.

And love—for ourselves as well as our Creator—is a strong motivator to help us conquer our fears.

· ·

Dear Papa God, Your endless love is amazing to me. Thank You that because of Your love, I have nothing to fear. Amen.

ATTITUDE OF GRATITUDE

*Come, let us sing to the L*ORD*! Let us shout joyfully to the Rock of our salvation. Let us come to him with thanksgiving. Let us sing psalms of praise to him.*

PSALM 95:1–2 NLT

Psalm 69:30; 147:7; Jonah 2:9; Colossians 2:7; 3:15–16; 4:2; Hebrews 12:28. If you take the time to look up these verses, you will see a pattern of thanksgiving.

I don't believe Papa God meant for us to thank only Him for the blessings that enrich our lives, but also to thank the people responsible for the little things that make our earthly sojourn more pleasant.

Sometimes an expression of gratitude can make all the difference in the world to people who need desperately to know that they count, that we value them. That their actions, however small, are appreciated. . .a harried waitress, the overworked clerk trying to whittle down a long waiting line, a lonely parking lot attendant, the day care worker up to her elbows in dirty diapers.

. . . .

Dear Papa God, my utmost thanksgiving and gratitude should be to You. Help me also to show gratitude to those You've placed around me. Amen.

POWERFUL THANKSGIVING

*Give thanks for everything to God the Father
in the name of our Lord Jesus Christ.*
EPHESIANS 5:20 NLT

Scientists, who in the past have generally disregarded the role of thankfulness, have now discovered that gratitude is one of the most powerful human emotions and can literally make people live longer, happier lives. In fact, gratitude journals are becoming a regular therapy tool used by many psychologists to help their clients reduce fearfulness, connect to others, and improve their emotional outlooks.

The idea is to recognize the people you're thankful for, consider what your life would be like without the things you enjoy, and be intentionally grateful for them. Then take it a step further and express your gratitude. The purpose is to morph your behavior from complaining to thankfulness, and a positive attitude adjustment will follow.

Isn't it terrific that psychology is finally catching on to what the Bible has told us for centuries?

. . . .

*Dear Papa God, there is such power
and peace in counting my blessings.
Thank You for all of them. Amen.*

THE LIFE REPAIRMAN

*Therefore, since we are surrounded by such
a huge crowd of witnesses to the life of faith,
let us strip off every weight that slows us down,
especially the sin that so easily trips us up. And let
us run with endurance the race God has set before
us. We do this by keeping our eyes on Jesus, the
champion who initiates and perfects our faith.*

HEBREWS 12:1–2 NLT

Dwelling on our problems is like staring day after day at the burned muffins, flopped quiche, and rock-hard cookies lining your counter rather than picking up the phone and calling the oven repairman. Addressing the source is the key, not lamenting about the symptoms. Call on the Life Repairman and tell Him not only your needs but what you appreciate about His handiwork. Praise Papa God for His loving attributes—patience, forgiveness, faithfulness, grace, healing, protection, provision, renewal, rest, security, and wisdom, to name a few—that He bestows on His beloved children. He's always willing to make a house call.

. . . .

Dear Papa God, You are all I need and the answer to every problem and question I have. Help me to run to You first and foremost for everything in my life. Amen.

ANSWERED PRAYER

Tell God what you need,
and thank him for all he has done.
PHILIPPIANS 4:6 NLT

I know that sometimes we don't feel thankful for God's answers, especially when troubles fill us with fear, anger, or resentment. But Papa God didn't specify that we should be thankful only for the good answers. No, He said to thank Him for all His answers, even when it's "No, My beloved child," "Wait on My perfect timing," or "I'm sorry you must go through this fire, precious one, but I will go through it with you." We don't have to feel happy about tough circumstances, but if we view the fire-treading moments when we're thankful-by-will-only as acts of faith, believing that our all-powerful, all-knowing Papa God is using even the grinding process of the tough times to sharpen our trust, we will draw closer to Him. And hey, isn't that our goal?

. . . .

Dear Papa God, Your answers to my prayers are
always good, whether they're what I'd hoped for
or not. Please help me to trust You more. Amen.

HOLD ON TIGHT

Shout with joy to the LORD, all the earth!
Worship the LORD with gladness. Come before him,
singing with joy. Acknowledge that the LORD is God!
He made us, and we are his. We are his people,
the sheep of his pasture. Enter his gates with
thanksgiving; go into his courts with praise. Give
thanks to him and praise his name. For the LORD
is good. His unfailing love continues forever, and
his faithfulness continues to each generation.

PSALM 100 NLT

Do you find it hard to hold tightly to thankfulness? When the hard times come—and they inevitably will—gratitude is one of the first things we lose our grip on. So grip harder. Counting our blessings in the midst of trouble is difficult, to be sure, but it's the very thing that will unknot our guts, calm our anguished hearts, lower our defenses, and melt our anger. We need to be grateful . . .not just spiritually but emotionally and physically too.

. . . .

Dear Papa God, hard circumstances often make me
forget all the blessings You've given. Please help me
to grip gratitude tightly. You are so good to me. Amen.

CHOOSE CONTENTMENT

Give thanks to the LORD, for he is good! His faithful love endures forever. Give thanks to the God of gods. His faithful love endures forever. Give thanks to the Lord of lords. His faithful love endures forever.

PSALM 136:1–3 NLT

Intentional choices, if practiced enough, become habits. Emulate the most thankful person you know. If no one comes to mind, you need a new crowd, girlfriend. Go out and meet someone whose countenance is joyful and whose eyes twinkle. Make no mistake—friends who do nothing but complain and gripe will drag you down. If you stand beneath a dripping faucet, you will get wet. You need to hang out with upbeat, positive people. In the meantime, fake it until it's real. You won't believe how fast purposely thinking and talking like you have a grateful spirit will actually produce one.

. . . .

Dear Papa God, I want to develop a constant habit of thankfulness. Please surround me with friends who want this too. Amen.

POWERFUL PROTECTION

We are not fighting against humans. We are fighting against forces and authorities and against rulers of darkness and powers in the spiritual world.

EPHESIANS 6:12 CEV

Did you know breastplates were also worn by high priests in Bible days to figuratively protect themselves from unrighteousness? *Righteousness* means "doing right in God's eyes"; those priestly guys were symbolically fending off the attacks of the enemy (Satan), which could very well result in sin and spiritual death.

Then—and now—wearing armor is a precaution to protect yourself from a wily, unscrupulous enemy. We may not use literal steel breastplates today, but we certainly need protection just as strong. You and I are still being attacked daily, although neither our enemy nor our armor is visible to the naked eye.

. . . .

Dear Papa God, please protect me and keep me strong in the fight against the enemy. I can withstand the attacks using the armor only You can give. Amen.

NOT AS WE DESERVE

He does not treat us as our sins deserve or repay us according to our iniquities. For as high as the heavens are above the earth, so great is his love for those who fear him; as far as the east is from the west, so far has he removed our transgressions from us. As a father has compassion on his children, so the LORD has compassion on those who fear him.

PSALM 103:10–13 NIV

Jesus Christ, the only truly innocent person who ever lived, was faced with the ultimate injustice: He was executed in a horrible, excruciatingly painful public debacle for something He didn't do. And He didn't fight it. He didn't scream and rant and rave about the unfairness of it all. He didn't even refuse to look at His offenders.

No. He looked at them all right—He looked right through them and saw raw, wounded, fallible humanity deep beneath the surface of their hateful actions. He compassionately asked God to forgive them because they didn't fully understand the grave atrocity they'd committed. And in doing so, Jesus forgave them too.

. . . .

Dear Papa God, I can never thank You enough for Your work on the cross to forgive my sins. Your compassion and love fill me with hope. Amen.

SEVENTY TIMES SEVEN

Then Peter came to him and asked, "Lord, how often should I forgive someone who sins against me? Seven times?" "No, not seven times," Jesus replied, "but seventy times seven!"
MATTHEW 18:21–22 NLT

Don't you agree that forgiveness is one of the most difficult things our faith requires of us? Most of us stink at it, but thankfully, it's a skill that improves with practice. The more we forgive, the more forgiving we become.

When we realize what forgiveness actually does for us, it's a wonder we don't jump to do it more often. Studies have shown that forgiveness decreases stress, depression, and anxiety. But that's really not news. Back in the sixteenth century, Martin Luther said, "Heavy thoughts bring on physical maladies; when the soul is oppressed, so is the body."

. . . .

Dear Papa God, You've made it very clear that I am to forgive others repeatedly, just as You forgive me. I can only do it with Your help. Thank You! Amen.

ONLY THE BRAVE

"If you forgive those who sin against you, your heavenly Father will forgive you. But if you refuse to forgive others, your Father will not forgive your sins."
MATTHEW 6:14–15 NLT

Forgiveness is essential to achieve inner peace. Grudges corrode the spirit. But you already know that. The longer we carry around grudges, the more ravenous they become as they devour our passion for life. Resentment is poisonous. The poison gradually spreads throughout every molecule of our being and slowly kills the life spark within us.

Like cancer of the soul.

Robert Muller, former assistant secretary-general of the United Nations, said, "Only the brave know how to forgive. A coward never forgives." I have to agree with that 100 percent. I can't think of anything more courageous than forgiving someone who has caused you harm. Especially on purpose.

. . . .

Dear Papa God, I don't want to carry grudges or hold on to past hurts. Please help me to be brave enough to forgive like You do. Amen.

CHOOSE TO OBEY ANYWAY

"If you have anything against someone, forgive—
only then will your heavenly Father be inclined
to also wipe your slate clean of sins."
MARK 11:25 MSG

How do we forgive? How do we release our need for revenge and prevent anger, bitterness, and resentment from raking our hearts with their destructive claws?

Well, one thing I've learned: you may not feel forgiving, but if, out of sheer obedience to Christ, you voice your pardon anyway—every day if need be, until it "takes" in your heart—true forgiveness will follow. In other words, feelings often come after the decision to take action. Mark Twain said, "In twenty years, you will be more disappointed by what you didn't do than by what you did."

So why not do it now and save yourself the angst?

. . . .

Dear Papa God, sometimes it seems
like forgiveness requires a constant battle
between my feelings and my actions. Help
me to act in obedience and trust You. Amen.

EMOTIONALLY WIRED

*Losing your temper causes a lot of trouble,
but staying calm settles arguments.*
PROVERBS 15:18 CEV

Emotions are wired into us by our passionate Father, who feels things strongly and made us in His image. We were created to feel. The only people who don't feel anger, bitterness, or resentment are dead people. But when we feel passionate emotions, we need to bring those potentially destructive emotions under Christ's submission and not let them run wild.

One way to do this is by writing down your negative feelings. Let them spill out freely—just vomit them all over the page. You then might consider taking it a step further by burning the paper or tying it to a helium balloon and releasing it in a symbolic gesture of letting your anger go. Something about watching that balloon float away on a gentle breeze is incredibly freeing.

Dear Papa God, my emotions feel so powerful sometimes, but Your Spirit and Your truth are always greater. Please help me to control my feelings in a way that pleases You. Amen.

RID YOURSELF OF RATS

*Be patient and trust the L*ORD*. Don't let it bother you when all goes well for those who do sinful things. Don't be angry or furious. Anger can lead to sin.*
PSALM 37:7–8 CEV

Harboring resentment is like chugging down strychnine and expecting the other person to die. Your anger doesn't hurt your offender. It hurts you. It wounds you and those who care about you, those who feel helpless and hopeless watching bitterness gnaw away like ravenous sewer rats at the you they love. Rats that will never be satiated.

I've heard it said that apologizing doesn't necessarily mean you're wrong and the other person is right. It just means you value relationships more than your ego. And isn't that the way Papa wants us to prioritize?

* *

Dear Papa God, please help me to resolve and let go of this resentment I'm holding. I don't want it to destroy my relationships with others and especially my relationship with You. Amen.

LET GOD CHANGE YOU

If you forgive others for the wrongs they do to you, your Father in heaven will forgive you. But if you don't forgive others, your Father will not forgive your sins.
MATTHEW 6:14–15 CEV

Forgiveness isn't about changing someone else. You don't have the power to do that. It's about changing something within you. You probably don't have the power to do that either, but you know Someone who does.

Forgiveness is about unlatching the hurt you wear like a heavy, bulletproof lead vest so that you can finally drop it to the floor and feel Papa God's big, loving, beating heart as He embraces you. He forgave you and wants you to do the same for others.

Forgiveness isn't really optional for believers—in order for us to receive forgiveness, we must give it. Forgiveness is the foundation for an ongoing intimate relationship with our heavenly Father. And He has good reason for issuing this ultimatum.

. . . .

Dear Papa God, please change my heart. Please soften it with a desire to forgive those who hurt me. I want to model Your forgiveness. Amen.

GRACE = AGGRESSIVE FORGIVENESS

Sin didn't, and doesn't, have a chance in competition with the aggressive forgiveness we call grace. When it's sin versus grace, grace wins hands down. All sin can do is threaten us with death, and that's the end of it. Grace, because God is putting everything together again through the Messiah, invites us into life.

ROMANS 5:20–21 MSG

Don't you just want to tattoo that incredible scripture right across your chest? (If yours is the size of mine, the words would wrap all the way around your back and down to your derriere dimples.)

Even after we make bad choices, grace invites us back into life. It won't leave us dead and rotting. It gives us the re-opportunity to live life to the fullest. Because grace, that "aggressive forgiveness" (I just love that phrase!), trumps sin. Any sin. And Papa God is already gluing the shattered pieces of the mess we've made of ourselves back together through the love of Jesus.

. . . .

Dear Papa God, thank You for gluing me back together again and again with Your grace. I don't even want to know where I'd be without it. Amen.

KEEP YOUR HELMET ON

*Take the helmet of salvation and the sword
of the Spirit, which is the word of God.*
EPHESIANS 6:17 NIV

"I think it all boils down to: Who are we going to trust?"
Marianna shared with me in her soft voice. "God knows
exactly what we think and feel. Peace comes in accepting
the path He's set out for us and realizing that none of
it was done to hurt us or make us miserable. We have
to trust that He'll fill in the holes."

You know, it's no coincidence that the piece of spiritual
armor representing salvation through grace is a helmet.
We need sturdy, impenetrable headgear to protect our
thoughts, reasoning, and motives from the destructive
fear of potential disaster. That thick brain padding in
our helmet is the assurance that through life, death, or
near misses, we're safe in Papa God's hands.

. . . .

*Dear Papa God, please help me to keep the helmet
of salvation always covering my head and thus my
thoughts, giving me constant confidence that I am
saved by You and safe in Your care. Amen.*

SWORD FIGHTING

For the word of God is alive and active. Sharper
than any double-edged sword, it penetrates even
to dividing soul and spirit, joints and marrow;
it judges the thoughts and attitudes of the heart.
HEBREWS 4:12 NIV

The ski-patrol guys who eventually found me wondered why I asked them to snap a photo of me before bundling me onto the rescue sled. "Are you sure this is a memory you want to keep?" one asked as he eyed my blue lips and swollen knee.

"Absolutely," I replied with assurance. "I always want to remember the day I learned to sword fight."

I'm a firm believer in the mega-importance of keeping a full arsenal of scripture loaded and ready for battle. God's Word is our sword—our biggest and best weapon. We never know when or where the enemy will ambush us, and we won't always have a Bible, our pastor, or our trusty notes handy. Our sword must be mobile, sharp, and handy at all times. Even on a lonely mountaintop.

. . . .

Dear Papa God, there is such power in Your Word,
power that I need to rely on in every battle, whether
internal or external, that I find myself in. Please help
me to memorize and live Your Word. Amen.

43

PERSONAL GPS

Your word is a lamp to guide
my feet and a light for my path.
PSALM 119:105 NLT

Two years ago, I became convicted that I needed to spend more daily time in the Word.

So I resolved to read, study, and meditate on scripture every single day, seven days a week. My reason was simple: I knew the Word was one of the primary ways Papa God speaks to us, and I didn't want to miss anything!

You know what? That decision has been the most edifying, beautifying, fulfilling decision of my life. I've heard something new and fresh and totally applicable from my Savior's still, small voice every day for the past two years. Scripture has become my life map, my guide, like a personal GPS (God-Powered Satellite).

• •

Dear Papa God, Your Word truly is a lamp
to my feet and a light to my path. It is such
a blessing to follow You. Amen.

YOU DON'T HAVE TO
BE OLIVE OYL

A final word: Be strong in the Lord and in his mighty power. Put on all of God's armor so that you will be able to stand firm against all strategies of the devil.
EPHESIANS 6:10–11 NLT

Hey, did you realize that the sword is the only piece of the armor of God that is an overtly offensive weapon? All the other armor components (shield, helmet, breastplate, chain mail, and boots) are primarily for defense and protection against assaults on us. The sword (scripture) is our designated weapon with which to aggressively attack and disarm our opponent. What kind of wimpy warriors would we be if all we could do is defend ourselves? We need to be willing and able to turn the tables and attack. I mean, really, who wants to be whiny Olive Oyl when you can be big, bad, bold Xena: Warrior Princess?

* *

Dear Papa God, help me remember I never need to be a wimpy Christian. You have equipped me with everything I need to be bold and brave for Your glory. Amen.

JUST CARETAKERS

*"I came naked from my mother's womb, and I will be naked when I leave. The L*ORD *gave me what I had, and the L*ORD *has taken it away. Praise the name of the L*ORD*!"*

JOB 1:21 NLT

You may not realize it, but finances are important to Papa God too. There are more than two thousand Bible verses about money and possessions. So we can be assured that He cares about the ins and outs of our economic situations (especially when there are more outs than ins).

When talking about money and what it buys, I think the first premise we must establish is that what little— or much—we own isn't really ours in the first place. We're just caretakers. "The earth and everything on it belong to the LORD" (Psalm 24:1 CEV). So although the bank account, trust fund, or mortgage might display our name, we're not the real owner. Papa God is.

· ·

Dear Papa God, every blessing I have ultimately comes from You. Please give me wisdom about my finances and open hands to give generously of what You've trusted to my care. Amen.

LEARN FROM MISTAKES

But now, O Jacob, listen to the L<small>ORD</small> who created
you. O Israel, the one who formed you says,
"Do not be afraid, for I have ransomed you.
I have called you by name; you are mine."

I<small>SAIAH</small> 43:1 <small>NLT</small>

The Old Testament children of Israel were chickenhearted about change. Time after time, as Moses was leading them away from their oppressive lives of Egyptian slave labor, they complained about having to adapt to the inconveniences of the journey. Moving forward into the unknown was more frightening than going back to their previous miserable but predictable existence. (See Exodus 16:3 and 17:3 for examples of their whining.)

In their cowardice, they did all sorts of stupid things: questioned God's power; disobeyed countless times; nearly stoned their deliverer, Moses; and built a golden calf to worship instead of almighty God.

C'mon, now. Of all things to promote into deity: a cow.

* *

Dear Papa God, please help me to learn from the
mistakes of the Israelites so that I can trust You
better, even in times of huge change. May the
Israelites also help me to learn how much You
love Your people, despite our mistakes. Amen.

47

GIVE UP CONTROL

"So do not worry, saying, 'What shall we eat?'
or 'What shall we drink?' or 'What shall we wear?'
For the pagans run after all these things, and
your heavenly Father knows that you need them.
But seek first his kingdom and his righteousness,
and all these things will be given to you as well."
MATTHEW 6:31–33 NIV

How many times have you, frantic over a looming major decision, called your BFF rather than hit your knees? Or believed something you read in a magazine over what you read in the Bible?

Count me guilty on that one too.

As I've said before and I'll say again, fear is really a control issue. We think if we can somehow maintain control over the things that happen to us, we'll be able to cruise along in happiness, peace, and tranquility. We may think we're in control, but the fact is, we've never been in control. And we never will be.

For some of us control addicts, that's the most frightening thought of all.

. . . .

Dear Papa God, I like to control things in my
own way, but Your ways are so much better.
Please help me to seek You first and give You
the steering wheel on every road I travel. Amen.

LOOSEN YOUR GRIP

*My God will meet all your needs according
to the riches of his glory in Christ Jesus.*

PHILIPPIANS 4:19 NIV

I love Elisabeth Elliot's perspective on gripping control too tightly: "Today is mine. Tomorrow is none of my business. If I peer anxiously into the fog of the future, I will strain my spiritual eyes so that I will not see clearly what is required of me now."

Face it, sister, you have no control over what creaks in the night, what others think of you, whether that other driver will start texting just as your daughter's car approaches, the longevity of your internal organs, the cruelty of the natural aging process, when your loved ones will be called to eternity, or a thousand other possibilities you can invent. You can't control what God does or doesn't do. Because He is God. He's the One in control. He always has been and always will be.

. . . .

Dear Papa God, I need a better balance of thinking wisely about the future yet not stressing over it or trying to control it. Please help me to live day by day, trusting You to provide and show me Your will. Amen.

WHEN WE DISOBEY GOD

This is love for God: to keep his commands.
And his commands are not burdensome.

1 JOHN 5:3 NIV

Saul, the tall, handsome donkey herder who was God's handpicked choice as the first king of Israel, repeatedly refused to obey the Almighty and was eventually rejected by the same hand that had crowned him (see 1 Samuel 16:1). God's Spirit left Saul and he was filled with depression and fear (see 1 Samuel 16:14).

Whoa. Let's stop right there for a moment and take note of what happens when disobedience separates us from the Spirit of the Lord: we are filled with depression and fear. This is a crucial point. Swipe it with your highlighter.

. . . .

Dear Papa God, I want to obey You in all things.
When I fail, please keep drawing me back to a right
relationship with You so that I can be filled with joy
and peace, not depression and fear. Amen.

WHY DOUBT?

He was terrified and began to sink. "Save me, Lord!"
he shouted. Jesus immediately reached out and
grabbed him. "You have so little faith,"
Jesus said. "Why did you doubt me?"
MATTHEW 14:30–31 NLT

"Why did you doubt Me?" That's the million-dollar question, isn't it? Why do we doubt Him when He's standing there in the middle of our sea of tribulation, proving to us that He's more than powerful enough to rise above the storm and hold us up there with Him? Why does it feel so much safer to crawl back into the boat?

Because we choose to listen to our toxic inner voices and become a boat-hugger when we could be a water-walker.

. . . .

Dear Papa God, my sinful inner voice and the
voices of others sometimes drag me down and
cause me to doubt You. Please help me to listen
and trust Your voice and Yours alone. Amen.

THE REAL ISSUES

But the Lord said to her, "My dear Martha, you are worried and upset over all these details! There is only one thing worth being concerned about. Mary has discovered it, and it will not be taken away from her."

LUKE 10:41–42 NLT

Jesus recognizes Martha's ruffled feelings—and in doing so, He validates that based on what's visible here, being upset is not an unrealistic response. But at the same time, He points out that emotions are not trustworthy. They're blocking Martha's view of the real issues. Provision for her guests is important, certainly, and so is respectful assistance from her family, but some things—nonphysical, can't-touch-this things—are even more important here: spiritual health, discovery of truth, relationships, salvation of your very soul. Things that need to be rated on an eternity continuum, not a daily checklist.

. . . .

Dear Papa God, please help me find that wise balance of doing what needs to be done in the here and now and yet always seeing things in the light of eternity. Amen.

HUMILITY PLUS GRATITUDE

Pride brings a person low,
but the lowly in spirit gain honor.
PROVERBS 29:23 NIV

In modern-day terms, Saul bit the hand that fed him. He completely forgot the piles of donkey poo he used to slog through in his pre-king days and neglected to be thankful for his blessings. He became self-centered and self-sufficient, no longer acknowledging the One responsible for his undeserved majesty, power, and lofty position. And worst of all, Saul grieved the heart of God by his willful disobedience (see 1 Samuel 15:11).

A fresh perspective of gratitude would have changed everything. Humility walking hand in hand with thankfulness likely would have created a desire within Saul to be obedient—and grateful—to the Source of his good fortune.

. . . .

Dear Papa God, I find myself so full of pride in
myself at times, and I'm sorry. Please forgive me
and help me to be humble and grateful for all
that You are and all that You do for me. Amen.

A RECORD OF HIS POWER

*"Remember the former things, those of
long ago; I am God, and there is no other;
I am God, and there is none like me."*
ISAIAH 46:9 NIV

We could all benefit from a prayer journal—a wonderful way to chronicle Papa God's power in our lives. So when doubt assaults our faith, fear threatens to devour us, and disaster hovers overhead like a cyclone, we'll be able to instantly recall the times when Papa God's merciful hands rescued us in astounding ways.

By remembering what Papa God has already done for us through Christ, we'll develop miracle memory. He defeated the instigator of fear at the cross, and He'll do it again. And again.

· ·

*Dear Papa God, You have been so good to me.
You've shown me Your love and blessings in so
many answered prayers. Remind me of them
daily so that I will trust You more. Amen.*

REALLY LIVING

*For God has not given us a spirit of fear and timidity,
but of power, love, and self-discipline.*
2 TIMOTHY 1:7 NLT

If we live in fear, the precious gift that you and I have been offered by the sacrifice Jesus made for us when He exchanged His life for ours is reduced to, well, gum on the sole of our Nike. Something we scrape off and throw away.

Instead of living unfettered, we anxiously calculate every risk. Freedom is exchanged for shackles. Boldness is trounced by cowardice. Joy is replaced by angst. Instead of moving forward in boldness, we hold back in timidity.

Living in fear is not really living at all.

. . . .

*Dear Papa God, I want to live confidently,
not fearfully, because of the Spirit of power, love, and
self-discipline You have given me. Thank You! Amen.*

THE THREAT OF LOSS

The righteous person may have many troubles,
*but the L*ORD *delivers him from them all.*

P*SALM* 34:19 N*IV*

Losing a loved one is a legitimate concern that will, sadly, happen to each of us at some point in our lives. But through Papa God's gift of power, love, and self-discipline, we don't have to be consumed by the threat of loss. Throwing away a priceless present like joy-filled freedom from fear is a slap in the face to the One who purchased it for us with His love.

Sure, the bad things we imagine *might* happen. Sometimes they *do* happen. Such is life. But is it better to shoot out our own lights and crawl under the covers in anticipation of nightfall, or dance in the sunlight and deal with the darkness when the sun goes down?

. . . .

Dear Papa God, the harsh realities in this fallen
world sometimes overwhelm me. Please comfort
me and remind me that You will make all things
right one day. Until then, help me live boldly
by Your powerful Spirit. Amen.

TRUE FREEDOM

*"If the Son makes you free,
you will be free indeed."*

JOHN 8:36 NASB

It's freedom we all want more than anything, isn't it? Freedom from the darkness of fear. Freedom from the threat of loss lurking at the edges of our minds. Freedom to throw our arms out wide as we live and laugh and love.

In order to find that freedom and effectively quench the darkness, we have to make the effort to reach upward toward the Source of all light and flip on the switch. Flood the room with light. Papa God's light. No bogeymen hanging out here! For God and fear cannot coexist in the same place; where His light shines, darkness vanishes. Fear is expelled by power, love, and self-discipline.

. . . .

*Dear Papa God, I want the power, love,
and self-discipline to live a truly free life that is
filled with Your light and brings You glory. Amen.*

GOD IS SOVEREIGN AND GOOD

*The LORD says: "My thoughts and my ways
are not like yours. Just as the heavens are
higher than the earth, my thoughts and
my ways are higher than yours."*
ISAIAH 55:8–9 CEV

It's awfully difficult to trust our Caretaker when we have experienced—or know someone who has experienced—devastating loss.

But the thing is, God's sovereignty is innately mysterious; He has the right to be unexplainable and unfathomable. He is God. I have this verse taped to my bathroom mirror to remind me of this: "The secret things belong to the LORD our God" (Deuteronomy 29:29 NIV).

Although death and loss are part of the cycle of life, Papa God's love for us remains strong and present. And where He is present, fear cannot be.

. . . .

*Dear Papa God, I don't always understand Your
ways, and there is such heartache in our world.
But You are sovereign and You are good,
and I will choose to trust You. Amen.*

GOD'S VIEW

"The LORD does not look at the things people look at. People look at the outward appearance, but the LORD looks at the heart."

1 SAMUEL 16:7 NIV

Even when we know better, we still tend to make snap judgments based on empirical evidence. We dis the one but respect the other before giving either a chance to prove him- or herself beneath the outside layer.

We don't bother to remove the wrapping paper before deciding whether we like the contents of the package.

Thankfully, Papa God doesn't think that way when He looks at us. The gifts the Lord specifically gives each of us are rarely on the surface. He has lovingly nestled virtues like discernment, kindness, or graciousness within our character.

. . . .

Dear Papa God, please give me eyes like Yours, eyes that discern the character inside people rather than judge by outer appearance. Amen.

ONE TRUE FOCUS

*Charm is deceptive, and beauty is fleeting;
but a woman who fears the LORD is to be praised.*
PROVERBS 31:30 NIV

When we're preoccupied with ourselves and our appearance, we're distracted from our one true focus: our God and Savior, Jesus Christ, and the people He has brought into our lives to be our special ministry. Our passion is directed inward rather than outward. Our bodies become like a god to us. But our Creator had something very important to say about that: "You shall have no other gods before Me" (Exodus 20:3 NKJV), the very first of the Ten Commandments.

No other gods. Just the one true capitalized God. Jehovah. Yahweh. I AM.

. . . .

Dear Papa God, I want You and You alone to receive my worship. Please draw me back to You when I stray toward focusing too much on myself and my appearance. Amen.

GOD'S BEAUTY STANDARDS

Don't be concerned about the outward beauty of fancy hairstyles, expensive jewelry, or beautiful clothes. You should clothe yourselves instead with the beauty that comes from within, the unfading beauty of a gentle and quiet spirit, which is so precious to God.

1 PETER 3:3–4 NLT

This is your therapy for today: repeat after me, "Mirrors are stupid!"

No, really, they are. Stupid, stupid, stupid. Mirrors don't know anything. They only tell us what we tell them to tell us. And that info is based on what others insist is acceptable or unacceptable through magazines, TV, infomercials, the internet, and movies. And remember, they're all trying to sell something!

How boring would we be without laugh-till-you-cry lines? And kindness crinkles? And love handles? And a little jowl jiggle to remind us of the scoop of ice cream we shared with that distraught friend?

That's beauty by God's measuring standard.

. . . .

Dear Papa God, Your standard of beauty is so much better than the standards of the world. I want to be beautiful in Your eyes only, and I'm so thankful for Your unconditional love. Amen.

A LINEAR PROCESS

For you created my inmost being; you knit me together in my mother's womb. I praise you because I am fearfully and wonderfully made.
PSALM 139:13–14 NIV

Viewing myself as ugly is a slap in the face to my Creator, who made me in His image. If I'm ugly, what does that make Him?

Beauty is a linear process. The process goes like this:

1. *Because of the affirmation I receive from my close relationship with Papa God, I feel loved.*
2. *Because I know I'm loved, I feel valued.*
3. *Because I rest in the assurance that I'm valued, I feel beautiful.*

Yes, that's right. At the risk of your thinking I'm a blind, arrogant diva, I'll say it again: I feel beautiful.

. . . .

Dear Papa God, when I'm feeling down about my appearance, please help me to remember that You created me in Your image. I am loved and gorgeous in Your eyes, and I am so grateful. Amen.

MAKE A PLAN AND KEEP IT

No discipline seems pleasant at the time,
but painful. Later on, however, it produces
a harvest of righteousness and peace for
those who have been trained by it.
HEBREWS 12:11 NIV

You and I both know that if we simply make vague promises to "do better" with our daily spiritual disciplines like prayer and Bible reading, we won't. It's just too easy to get caught up in the bustle and confusion of everyday life and lose sight of our vision and goals.

We end up taking care of everyone but ourselves.

Sure, it's great when we vow to make changes on both spiritual and physical planes: to read our Bibles every day, "pray without ceasing" (1 Thessalonians 5:17 NKJV), make healthier eating choices, and limit our food intake. But if we don't make a plan and then diligently work that plan, it just won't happen.

We definitely need discipline.

. . . .

Dear Papa God, I need major help with
discipline in my spiritual and physical health
since it's so easy to fall back into comfortable
habits. I want to make commitments and keep
them. I can with Your power. Amen.

ALWAYS WORTH IT

*I discipline my body like an athlete, training it to do
what it should. Otherwise, I fear that after preaching
to others I myself might be disqualified.*

1 CORINTHIANS 9:27 NLT

You don't simply wish for dinner and then sit back and
wait for it to magically appear, do you? Well, come
to think of it, I do. . .but you shouldn't. You plan your
menu, do the shopping, prepare the food, and then pop
it into the oven. Otherwise you'd end up with a growling
tummy and an empty plate.

It's the same with both spiritual and physical fitness.
No one ever said discipline is easy, but the end results
(spiritual muscles of steel and a tight tush instead of
cauliflower buns) are absolutely worth it.

* *

*Dear Papa God, help me to realize that wise
discipline for good spiritual and physical
health is always worth it, no matter how hard
it might seem in the midst of it. Amen.*

LOVED NO MATTER WHAT

May you have the power to understand, as all God's people should, how wide, how long, how high, and how deep his love is. May you experience the love of Christ, though it is too great to understand fully. Then you will be made complete with all the fullness of life and power that comes from God.

EPHESIANS 3:18–19 NLT

Our outsides are not always reflections of our insides. You can look great but feel wretched. Botoxed on the outside but crinkle fried on the inside. It doesn't matter that your teeth are straight if your attitude is warped. There's no magical cure for discontentedness or lagging self-esteem. If God's peace isn't in your heart when you're heavy, it won't be there when you're thin either.

After all, God loves Sumo wrestlers just as much as runway models!

. . . .

Dear Papa God, I'll never understand it fully, but I want to be aware of Your amazing love constantly. There's nothing I can do or become to earn it—You just love me unconditionally. There is such peace and joy in knowing that. Thank You! Amen.

BEAUTY THAT LASTS

Charm is deceptive, and beauty does not last;
but a woman who fears the LORD will be greatly
praised. Reward her for all she has done.
Let her deeds publicly declare her praise.

PROVERBS 31:30–31 NLT

Sometimes it's hard to remember that nurturing a gentle and quiet spirit is more important than "chasing the latest fashions" as the apostle Paul warns in 1 Timothy 2:10 (MSG). We fashion-chasers tend to buy into the image-is-everything propaganda our culture feeds us and have somehow intertwined physical appearance with affirmation of self-worth.

As if our personal value depends on how well we accessorize.

Paul was absolutely right when he said the way we really become beautiful is by doing something beautiful for God. Regardless of our appearance—how well we decorate this earth suit we've been assigned for a short time—true beauty answers to a higher, more exalted standard than bangle bracelets or tulle overlays.

. . . .

Dear Papa God, I want true, lasting beauty
not the superficial, temporary kind. Please
help me remember that real beauty results
from fearing and serving You. Amen.

TRULY ATTRACTIVE

Women who claim to be devoted to
God should make themselves attractive
by the good things they do.
1 TIMOTHY 2:10 NLT

No one will ever be more beautiful than Mother Teresa. Or Corrie ten Boom. Or Nellie Poss Rogers (my grandmother). Women who never wore diamond necklaces or silk camisoles or strappy heels in their lives, but who radiated ethereal beauty that the accessories of this world can't possibly mimic.

So the next time I'm trying on shorts, instead of succumbing to hopeless despair, I plan to dwell on the beautiful things I'm doing for God and let the cellulite fall where it may.

. . . .

Dear Papa God, please lessen my desire for what
popular culture says is beautiful, and help me to
desire the kind of beauty like that of heroic women
of the faith, both past and present. Amen.

HIS MASTERPIECE

*Oh yes, you shaped me first inside, then out;
you formed me in my mother's womb. I thank you,
High God—you're breathtaking! Body and soul,
I am marvelously made! I worship in adoration—
what a creation! You know me inside and out,
you know every bone in my body; you know
exactly how I was made, bit by bit, how I was
sculpted from nothing into something.*

PSALM 139:13–15 MSG

Makeup itself is not a problem; God wants us to present ourselves as the best we can be.

The real issue is our dependency upon augmentation of our God-given appearance for acceptance and self-esteem, whether through makeup, surgical alterations, or high fashion. How dependent are we on external fixes to feel that we fit in? Are accepted? Are attractive? He created us, each and every one a masterpiece, in our natural state, rough-hewn and raw. And He loves us lavishly just that way.

. . . .

*Dear Papa God, help me to truly believe that
You have made me beautiful and that You have
created me uniquely and wonderfully. I want my
self-esteem to come from You alone. Amen.*

AUTHENTICALLY EMULATING CHRIST

"You hypocrites! Isaiah was right when he prophesied about you, for he wrote, 'These people honor me with their lips, but their hearts are far from me. Their worship is a farce, for they teach man-made ideas as commands from God.'"

MATTHEW 15:7–9 NLT

If I'm serious about emulating Christ, there shouldn't be a difference between my inward and outward image. My Christian persona should be the real deal, not just for show.

It's an uncomfortable subject for most Christians—this double-life conundrum. We don't like to admit that yes, well, maybe sometimes we do tend to put on the dog. The show dog. To yell at our families at home and then appear at church like Laura Bush on Xanax. To cheat on our taxes while teaching in Sunday school that stealing is wrong. To proclaim to our kids that Jesus wants us to love our neighbor as ourselves and then scream hair-curling jerk-scenities behind the steering wheel.

. . . .

Dear Papa God, I want to be an authentic servant of You. Please forgive me when I mess this up, and help me do better at emulating You, inside and out, every day. Amen.

DON'T BE A SHOW DOG

"Woe to you, teachers of the law and Pharisees, you hypocrites! You shut the door of the kingdom of heaven in people's faces. You yourselves do not enter, nor will you let those enter who are trying to."
MATTHEW 23:13–14 NIV

Jesus confronted the vileness of hypocrisy in Matthew 23:13–39 (NIV). He lamented, "Woe to you," no less than seven times in this single chapter and associated being a show dog with the terms "blind guides," "snakes," and "brood of vipers."

Strong words. Make no mistake: the Almighty has strong feelings about this subject.

So where is our disconnect? Could it be that we live double lives because we're simply unwilling to surrender all facets of ourselves to God? To hand over all our masks? Maybe it's a pride issue. We want to decide which mask we'll wear and for whom. Concealing our true selves becomes our secret shame, and we end up as show dogs. With fleas.

. . . .

Dear Papa God, I want to surrender
every area of my life so that my
true self is true to You. Amen.

YOUR BEST YOU

God planned for us to do good things and to live as he has always wanted us to live. That's why he sent Christ to make us what we are.

EPHESIANS 2:10 CEV

There's not a thing wrong with presenting the best "you" possible. God is pleased when we respect His handiwork enough to put our prettiest toenails forward.

The problem arises when we become consumed with manipulating our image to control what other people think of us. Control is the key word here. We're really fighting the Lord for control when we're obsessing about how we appear to others. It becomes all about impressing other weak humans like us, not proudly expressing the brushstrokes of the masterpiece that Papa God purposefully created in us.

. . . .

Dear Papa God, please help me both to present my best self and to humbly give You the glory, not to impress others or to try to control what they think about me. Amen.

WHAT LOOK ARE YOU GOING FOR?

"God doesn't require attention-getting devices."
MATTHEW 6:18 MSG

We all struggle to keep our eyes on the Creator and not on the created (ourselves). I actually cringed when a man in my couples Bible study group commented, "My, Debbie, you look very wholesome tonight."

Wholesome? That was not the look I was going for. Attractive, lovely, feminine, ravishing—even color-coordinated would have been welcomed. But wholesome? Isn't cracked wheat wholesome?

Then the more I thought about it, I realized that was actually one of the nicest compliments I've ever received. Wholesome is precisely the way Papa God desires for me to be perceived, especially by men who aren't my husband.

· ·

Dear Papa God, in such a self-centered world, I need help with wanting to attract people to You not to myself. You should always be the look I'm going for. Please let Your light shine bright in me. Amen.

BUILD OTHERS UP

Let no unwholesome word proceed from your mouth, but only such a word as is good for edification according to the need of the moment, so that it will give grace to those who hear.
Ephesians 4:29 NASB

The apostle Paul correlates wholesomeness with the "edification" of others in Ephesians 4:29 (NASB). The definition of *edification* is "improvement in morality." So what Paul is saying is that we should present ourselves to others in a way that improves them—builds up their character—not only by our appearance but in our speech and actions as well.

That means no pretenses, false fronts, or role-playing to build ourselves up in the eyes of others. Why? Because our focus is on them not us.

Wow—what a relief! How much easier to be one person. . .inside and out. . .to any audience. . .at all times.

. . . .

Dear Papa God, please help me to be authentic to all those around me, no matter who I'm with, and let me build them up and lead them closer to You. Amen.

GOD SEES YOU

The Lord *looks down from heaven and sees the whole human race. From his throne he observes all who live on the earth. He made their hearts, so he understands everything they do.*

Psalm 33:13–15 NLT

Do you too ever feel invisible? Like life is swirling all around you, but you aren't included? Like people look right through you as if you're not worth focusing on?

When we feel invisible, we often pretend it doesn't matter for the sake of self-preservation. That's how we keep our sanity and don't run screaming into the night. But it does matter. It matters to us and it matters to God, who created us for significance.

"How precious are your thoughts about me, O God. They cannot be numbered! I can't even count them; they outnumber the grains of sand!" (Psalm 139:17–18 NLT).

. . . .

Dear Papa God, sometimes I feel like I don't matter much, but Your Word reminds me that is never true. Thank You for seeing me and loving me and having good plans for me. Amen.

NO NEED FOR LABELS

For God made Christ, who never sinned, to be the offering for our sin, so that we could be made right with God through Christ.
2 CORINTHIANS 5:21 NLT

Labels can build us up or tear us down. Some women wear a chic label proudly. Others work hard to earn labels like professional, successful, or competent. Still others become known by their beliefs as pro-life, godly, activist, or conservative.

We rely on labels to clarify our identity. If we're not sure who we really are—or maybe don't like who we really are—we can hide behind a designer label that reflects who we wish we were.

But God doesn't believe in labels. When we invite Jesus into our hearts and ask Him to fill us with His love, all God sees when He looks at us is the gentle, sweet, beautiful reflection of His Son.

. . . .

Dear Papa God, I'm so grateful for salvation and a right relationship with You because of Jesus' sacrifice for my sins. Thank You, thank You, thank You! Amen.

A RICH NEW IDENTITY

Anyone who belongs to Christ is a new person.
The past is forgotten, and everything is new.
2 CORINTHIANS 5:17 CEV

When you ask Jesus to fill you with His presence, you have a new identity; a pure, healthy, holy, confident identity. The old labels are obsolete. It's like intentionally enrolling in the witness protection program—you get to begin anew in the richness of your identity in Christ.

Now, c'mon, girl, start afresh! It's a brand-new day. Hold your head up. You're not faux Prada or Gucci or Ralph Lauren anymore; you're the unique, gorgeous real thing! Proudly wear the label of the Master Designer!

. . . .

Dear Papa God, I accept You as my Savior,
and I want You to make me new. I need a fresh
start and forgiveness and freedom from my sin,
as only You can provide. Now that I've accepted
You, my identity is always found in You—that's
so amazing and awesome! Amen.

LOVED AND LOVELY

Though outwardly we are wasting away,
yet inwardly we are being renewed day by day.
2 CORINTHIANS 4:16 NIV

God's values and the world's are just the opposite. It's our inside-out kind of beauty that's most important to Him—the only thing of eternal value. Even so, sometimes we all wrestle with keeping our attention focused on God and not on designer jeans. Especially if there's a sale at Macy's.

Real beauty comes only from God's inside-out love. When we finally comprehend His extravagant and intimate love for us, from our flat feet to our split ends, then our heart-glow will reflect radiant beauty from the inside out. We'll finally feel beautiful.

Only when we feel truly loved are we free to feel truly lovely.

* *

Dear Papa God, please fill me with Your
love. Let it be evident in me—let it be the
source of my beauty, a beauty that will
never deteriorate or diminish. Amen.

FOR GOD'S GLORY

We take captive every thought to
make it obedient to Christ.
2 CORINTHIANS 10:5 NIV

It's really a good thing to make the most of our appearance; I believe God is pleased when our motivation is to be the best we can be to reflect the glory of our Creator. The problem arises when our motivation insipidly morphs into reflecting our own glory: the glory of the created. Then we risk becoming obsessive fashionistas. Coveting becomes a way of life. Jealousy flares. Greed flourishes. Stress escalates.

Our inside-out focus reverses to outside-in; we lose sight of our upward purpose and fall into a downward spiral.

But, sister, take heart! Striking a spiritually healthy balance is possible. It just takes conviction and effort—like anything worthwhile. Lassoing and corralling our rogue cravings is an important part of maturing spiritually.

. . . .

Dear Papa God, it's a daily struggle not to do things
for my own glory. Please help my attitudes and
actions to bring praise to You and You alone. Amen.

A MUCH-NEEDED SPATULA

Finally, brothers and sisters, whatever is true, whatever is noble, whatever is right, whatever is pure, whatever is lovely, whatever is admirable—if anything is excellent or praiseworthy—think about such things.

PHILIPPIANS 4:8 NIV

Taking greedy thoughts captive doesn't happen in one fell swoop. It's a process, much like the process used by the candymaker I observed in a quaint chocolate shoppe during a mountain vacation. The skilled craftswoman worked the thickening fudge constantly until it was ready to mold into its finished form.

Our thoughts are like that unformed fudge. Left on their own, they'd spread out everywhere, oozing over the edges of God's parameters until they ended up a nasty, useless mess on the floor. But with a spatula of consistent guidance and discipline, we can scoop up our rogue thoughts and rework them into something valuable, beneficial, and delicious.

* * *

Dear Papa God, You know my thoughts and You know I need help controlling them. I want them to be pleasing to You, and I want to clear my mind of anything that grieves You. Amen.

READY TO FIGHT

"Watch and pray so that you will not fall into temptation. The spirit is willing, but the flesh is weak."
MATTHEW 26:41 NIV

Temptation seizes us in its vise-grip talons like a gigantic pterodactyl swooping in, plucking us out of our safe, warm nests, and flying away with us.

We don't have to helplessly succumb. We can fight back!

My foolproof way to escape a temptation attack is to keep prayer lists in my purse and car so that when those talons begin piercing my skin over that enticing dress or cute hat, I'm prepared. I pull out my prayer list and turn my attention to the needs of others. My focus shifts off my petty desires and onto those for whom I desire to be Christ's hands and feet. The wicked pterodactyl releases me. Works every time!

. . . .

Dear Papa God, temptation is a strong force, but Your Word is stronger. Please help me to avoid temptation, and when I do experience it, please help me to be ready to fight it and beat it! Amen.

THE BEST BEAUTY ADVICE

I pray that God, the source of hope, will fill you completely with joy and peace because you trust in him. Then you will overflow with confident hope through the power of the Holy Spirit.

ROMANS 15:13 NLT

Fill your mind with prayer and your spirit will be exalted. That's true beauty shining from the inside out! In *Beauty by the Book*, author and TV celebrity Nancy Stafford puts it so well: "The best beauty advice isn't about the latest beauty products and has nothing to do with anything you buy or apply. It has to do with the inner radiance that comes from a tended-to spirit and joy-filled experiences."

So when that beauty beast tries to take a bite out of your hide or impale you with his razor-sharp talons, be prepared. Kick him in the teeth (with your best pointy-toed boots) and send him yelping.

. . . .

Dear Papa God, when I'm comparing myself to what culture says is beautiful, please remind me that nothing is more attractive than a peaceful spirit and a joyful smile that come from You. Amen.

DESIRE DISCERNMENT

*You have dealt well with Your servant, O LORD,
according to Your word. Teach me good discernment
and knowledge, for I believe in Your commandments.*
PSALM 119:65–66 NASB

Spiritual discernment is extremely important for Christ-followers. So important that the Bible says we should desire it. Yearn for it. Pray for more.

What exactly is spiritual discernment? It's the ability to analyze, understand, and judge from an enlightened perspective what is and is not from God. Because the Lord knew how confused we can get when we're inundated with things not from God in the course of our every day, He sent a Helper—the Holy Spirit—to enable us to distinguish the difference.

. . . .

*Dear Papa God, with so many differing
viewpoints today about the meaning of Your
Word, I desperately need discernment that
comes from You alone. Help me to hear Your
voice, do Your will, and share Your love. Amen.*

SUPERNATURAL GOOGLE

The Spirit searches all things,
even the deep things of God.
1 CORINTHIANS 2:10 NIV

The Greek word *apolalupto* (from which apocalypse is derived) means "to pull the covers back; to make bare" and is used in this passage to describe how the Holy Spirit empowers us for discernment.

He pulls back the covers. He exposes lies. And when worldly untruth masquerading as God's truth is uncovered, its nakedness is hideous indeed.

In modern vernacular, the Holy Spirit is our spiritual search engine. Our supernatural Google. Because our own world-diluted judgment isn't altogether trustworthy, we must tap into His vast database of truth versus clever lies in order to practice good spiritual discernment.

· ·

Dear Papa God, I don't want Google to be my go-to for every kind of question. I want Your Spirit to give me answers and guide me through life. Amen.

BE PICKY-CHOOSY

And this is my prayer: that your love may abound more and more in knowledge and depth of insight, so that you may be able to discern what is best and may be pure and blameless for the day of Christ, filled with the fruit of righteousness that comes through Jesus Christ—to the glory and praise of God.

PHILIPPIANS 1:9–11 NIV

God wants us to be picky-choosy about what we do; where we go; whom we hang with; what we feed our eyes, ears, and minds; and even (shudder!) what we put into our mouths. Good discernment is crucial; the choices we make today will affect all of our tomorrows.

But the encouraging news is that we're not on our own. We have the Holy Spirit as our helper. Charles Spurgeon said, "Discernment is not a matter of simply telling the difference between right and wrong; rather it is telling the difference between right and almost right."

. . . .

Dear Papa God, I need to be extremely picky-choosy in a selfish, sinful world. So many things could keep me far from You. Please give me wisdom and discernment to make good choices and keep close to You. Amen.

JUST NOT CUTTING IT

"Come to me, all you who are weary and burdened, and I will give you rest. Take my yoke upon you and learn from me, for I am gentle and humble in heart, and you will find rest for your souls. For my yoke is easy and my burden is light."
MATTHEW 11:28–30 NIV

The temptation to forgo our daily God time is strong these days, yet the busier we are, the more we need the inner peace that only He can give.

I think we all reach a point in our lives when fifteen minutes of quiet time in the morning just isn't cutting it. We've lost touch with our first love: Christ. We're exhausted physically, frazzled emotionally, and parched spiritually. We need an extended time of renewal in every sense of the word.

. . . .

Dear Papa God, I crave an extended retreat with You to renew and refresh our relationship. Please help me to make the time. Amen.

AWAY FROM THE HUSTLE

*"To whom will you compare me? Or who is my equal?"
says the Holy One. Lift up your eyes and look to the
heavens: Who created all these? He who brings out
the starry host one by one and calls forth each of
them by name. Because of his great power
and mighty strength, not one of them is missing.*
Isaiah 40:25–26 NIV

There are numerous examples in scripture of Jesus
stealing away alone for prayer and renewal; some of
His favorite retreat sites were the mountains (see Mark
6:46) and the seaside or lake (see Matthew 13:1). I
believe that's because He knew our Father's pure,
unmarred creation—away from the hustle and bustle
of everyday life—is the most conducive environment in
which to commune with the heart of the Creator.

. . . .

*Dear Papa God, Your power and glory are so
clear in the quiet majesty of Your creation.
Please help me to get away from the stress
of life and commune with You. Amen.*

LIFE'S SINKHOLES

The one who is in you is greater
than the one who is in the world.

1 JOHN 4:4 NIV

There are times in all of our lives when we feel as though we've been swallowed by a sinkhole. Something shakes our world, and the ground beneath our feet falls away. Our sense of normalcy is disrupted and our foundation of security splits wide open, leaving us staring up from the bottom of a deep pit at the life we once knew.

We need to have a dependency on something—or Someone—larger and more powerful than ourselves to lift us out. In fact, the more independent we become, the more likely we are to stubbornly keep wallowing in our sinkholes.

· ·

Dear Papa God, when I find myself stuck
and helpless, it's all the more reason to be
dependent on You. Please strengthen and
lift me as only You can. Amen.

ALWAYS NEAR

Rejoice in the Lord always. I will say it again: Rejoice! Let your gentleness be evident to all. The Lord is near. Do not be anxious about anything, but in every situation, by prayer and petition, with thanksgiving, present your requests to God.
PHILIPPIANS 4:4–6 NIV

As a child, I used to have dreadful nightmares. I would awaken in the middle of the night, terrified and sweat-soaked. In a panic, I'd cry out for my father, who I knew was just in the next room. Within seconds, Daddy would be there, stroking my back, whispering soft words of comfort, and soothing me back to peaceful rest.

Philippians 4:5 (NIV) reminds us that "the Lord is near." Even closer than a loving earthly father, our heavenly Father is standing by to soothe, comfort, and reassure us.

. . . .

Dear Papa God, You are always near. I'm the one who creates distance between us at times. Please forgive me of my sins and draw me close to You. Amen.

SUPERNATURAL MR. CLEAN

[The Lord] said, "My grace is all you need.
My power works best in weakness." So now
I am glad to boast about my weaknesses,
so that the power of Christ can work through
me. . . . For when I am weak, then I am strong.
2 CORINTHIANS 12:9–10 NLT

God's divine intervention is more obvious when I'm a pathetic basket case. Which is most of the time. He then gets full credit for being God. For making the incredible difference.

Women certainly understand this principle; we know a filthy, wadded-up shirt is totally transformed when washed and ironed. No kitchen floor is cleaner than the one previously covered with muddy footprints! No legs appear smoother than those finally shaved after two weeks of neglect.

It's the same when our own efforts at cleaning up the embedded stains in our character fall short. We simply can't scrub that hard. Only our supernatural Mr. Clean can.

. . . .

Dear Papa God, my weaknesses highlight Your
strength and power and make me depend on You.
Help me not to hate my shortcomings but to praise
You for them. Amen.

THE ROVER PERSPECTIVE

See what great love the Father has lavished
on us, that we should be called children
of God! And that is what we are!

1 JOHN 3:1 NIV

If only we could see ourselves through the Rover perspective.

Picture yourself rolling out of bed in the morning. You are grumpy, frumpy, with bed hair, dragon breath, and no makeup. But what does your precious doggie do when he sees you? He wags himself into a frenzy. He's chock-full of slobbery, devoted, unconditional adoration. For you. In his eyes, you are the most beautiful person in the world. Rover loves you; he sees you, the real spirit-core you, not what you own or what you look like.

We need to start viewing ourselves like Rover does: entirely loved and entirely lovable.

God certainly sees us that way.

* *

Dear Papa God, I don't ever have to pretend to be
something I'm not with You. You know and love me
far more than any person or pet. Please give me
confidence in Your great love for me. Amen.

NOBODY'S PERFECT

For we do not have a high priest who is unable to empathize with our weaknesses, but we have one who has been tempted in every way, just as we are— yet he did not sin. Let us then approach God's throne of grace with confidence, so that we may receive mercy and find grace to help us in our time of need.
HEBREWS 4:15–16 NIV

None of us is perfect. Flaws will always be with us. But that doesn't mean we aren't lovely in our own right and shouldn't hold our heads up and share the gifts and abilities we do have.

I don't want to be sold out to fear of inadequacy or to society's standards of worth. Do you? No way! We'd rather be "souled" out to the Master Creator who made us in His image and cherishes us.

. . . .

Dear Papa God, I am not perfect, and that's okay, because You are! And despite my flaws, You have given me awesome gifts and abilities to share with others. Thank You for understanding and cherishing me. Amen.

SUPERNATURAL GRACE

*Be strong in the grace that
is in Christ Jesus.*
2 TIMOTHY 2:1 NIV

We all make mistakes—some knowingly, some not. We inadvertently hurt people at times. We let people down, trample feelings, don't live up to expectations. But it's not just careless or bad behavior at stake. Make no mistake, sister, guilt is a spiritual battle.

Many of us are spiritually schizophrenic like the apostle Paul in Romans 7:15 (MSG): "What I don't understand about myself is that I decide one way, but then I act another, doing things I absolutely despise."

And then guilt sets in like wet cement.

Even when we ask forgiveness, sometimes our guilt brakes don't engage, and self-persecution just keeps barreling full speed ahead. That's when we have to allow Papa God to override the gears and stall out our revving self-condemnation engine with His supernatural grace.

. . . .

*Dear Papa God, I'm so tired of letting guilt
control me. Please override the gears of
my guilt with Your amazing grace. Amen.*

LIKE PIGS IN MUD

For his unfailing love toward those who fear him is as great as the height of the heavens above the earth. He has removed our sins as far from us as the east is from the west.
PSALM 103:11–12 NLT

We do ourselves no favors by rolling like little pigs in the mud of guilt over our mistakes. Staying in the pigsty is not what God intends for us to do. Once we ask forgiveness for our wrongs, He wants to morph us from filthy piglets into majestic eagles so that we can soar high above the nasty mud holes, our wings supported by His very breath.

It's just plain dumb to refuse the wings and keep our snouts immersed in slop.

. . . .

Dear Papa God, please remind me how far You remove my sins from me. I don't want to wallow in them like mud when I could bask in Your loving grace instead. Amen.

SPECIAL GRACE NOTES

The heavens proclaim the glory of God. The skies display his craftsmanship. Day after day they continue to speak; night after night they make him known.

PSALM 19:1–2 NLT

If you're like me, although I'm usually focused on my urgent agenda, I occasionally sneak up on myself and actually see something I've never really seen before even though I've encountered it a million times. But this time I see it with my heart. . .before my pragmatic self can talk me out of it.

The exquisite artistry of a dew-glistened spiderweb, misty early-morning sunbeams reaching toward earth like the Almighty's fingers, the funny antics of a roly-poly puppy—all these things pour refreshing beauty into our thirsty hearts and bring a moment of sweet rest to our weary souls. They're Papa God's special grace notes. Ralph Waldo Emerson said, "Never lose an opportunity of seeing anything beautiful, for beauty is God's handwriting."

. . . .

Dear Papa God, please help me not to get so wrapped up in myself and my agenda that I miss how You're speaking to me in beautiful ways every day. Amen.

SPIRITUAL VITAMINS

"Study this Book of Instruction continually. Meditate on it day and night so you will be sure to obey everything written in it. Only then will you prosper and succeed in all you do."
JOSHUA 1:8 NLT

An excellent spiritual booster is to meditate on one simple scripture per day. A good verse to start with is Colossians 2:10 (NASB): "In Him you have been made complete." Jot the verse down, take it with you, and repeat it to yourself throughout the day, considering all implications and possible meanings. By the end of the month, you'll have studied thirty different scriptures and will be amazed at how personal the Word has become. (Hint: The book you're holding is full of brief, meaty verses you can use!)

Other effective spiritual vitamins include reading faith-based books, listening to uplifting music, and getting together with Christian friends.

. . . .

Dear Papa God, so much more important than vitamins for my physical health are "vitamins" for my spiritual health. Please help me to make a habit of wanting daily doses of You and Your Word. Amen.

BE STILL

"Be still, and know that I am God."
PSALM 46:10 NIV

Many times I'm too busy to allow my heavenly Father to snuggle with me. His arms are open wide, but I fill up my day with checking emails, shopping, working, cleaning, cooking—all the while running over for a token high five or peck on the cheek via a microwave prayer before leaving Him standing there as I return alone to life as I know it.

And then eventually, operating on my own strength, I run out of gas. Maybe Papa God actually wants me to finally run out of energy so that I'll sink into His lap and not fight the rejuvenation He longs to give me. What kind of crazy woman would actually resist resting in the arms of the One who loves her more than life itself?

. . . .

Dear Papa God, You long to love and comfort me, and I too often ignore how much I need that. Please help me choose to stop and relax in the rest and relief that only You can give. Amen.

A LOVING TIP

[God] comforts us when we are in trouble,
so that we can share that same
comfort with others in trouble.
2 CORINTHIANS 1:4 CEV

So wassup in your sinkhole? Are you wallowing or climbing? Festering or forging a trail upward?

When you're sick to death of clinging by your fingernails to those steep walls, just let go. Stretch your arms up and ask for Someone to reach a strong hand down to pull you up. He will, you know. You don't have to do it alone.

Philippians 4:5 (NIV) reminds us "the Lord is near." Even closer than a loving earthly father, our heavenly Father is standing by to soothe, comfort, and reassure us.

And haul us out of our lonely sinkholes.

. . . .

Dear Papa God, thank You for Your awesome
love—a love even greater than my earthly father
has for me. Help me to remember that I'm never
alone, even when life gets scary and hard. Amen.

GOD'S ANSWERING MACHINE

This is the confidence we have in approaching God: that if we ask anything according to his will, he hears us. And if we know that he hears us—whatever we ask—we know that we have what we asked of him.

1 John 5:14–15 NIV

Johan van der Dong created God's Hotline, which informed the caller, "This is the voice of God. I am not able to speak to you at the moment, but please leave a message."

We leave messages on God's answering machine too, don't we? When we have something to say, it's easy to pick up the celestial hotline and spill, but somehow it's much more difficult to expect a reply.

Could it be that deep down inside we're afraid God might not answer? That He'll put us on hold indefinitely and forget about us? Maybe we think He's just too busy solving world hunger and preventing wars to take time for us. Or maybe we don't feel worthy of His attention.

But we couldn't be more wrong.

- -

Dear Papa God, Your Word says You hear and answer anything we ask according to Your will. Thank You! Please help me to know and follow Your will more closely. Amen.

NEVER STOP PRAYING

Let your hope make you glad. Be patient in time of trouble and never stop praying.
Romans 12:12 CEV

Scripture offers many reasons why we should pray: to increase our wisdom and understanding (Ephesians 1:17–18), to glorify God and to strengthen ourselves and other believers (2 Thessalonians 1:11–12), and to share our faith (Philemon 6). The Bible even recommends where and when we should pray:

- *Day or night (Psalm 42:8)*
- *In the throes of busyness and in peace (1 Thessalonians 5:17)*
- *Amid trouble (Jonah 2:1)*
- *In private (Matthew 6:6; Luke 5:16)*
- *Away from home to avoid distractions, preferably a place surrounded by God's handiwork, such as the sea or a mountaintop (Luke 22:39–41; Mark 6:46)*

Dear Papa God, there is never a time or reason I should not be praying. Help me to realize that I can and should be in constant conversation with You. Amen.

STILL, SMALL VOICE

Behold, the LORD passed by, and a great and strong wind rent the mountains, and brake in pieces the rocks before the LORD; but the LORD was not in the wind: and after the wind an earthquake; but the LORD was not in the earthquake: and after the earthquake a fire; but the LORD was not in the fire: and after the fire a still small voice.

1 KINGS 19:11–12 KJV

God gave the prophet Elijah a very memorable object lesson about prayer. While escaping wicked Queen Jezebel, Elijah was exposed to some of Earth's most powerful forces of nature. Gale-force winds, an earthquake, and finally a monstrous fire.

But the Lord's presence wasn't in any of those things. Nope. Too crazy. Too noisy. Too overwhelming. To Elijah's surprise, God was in the still, small voice that came only in the quiet after the storms. No doubt he had to strain to hear it after all that racket.

Sound anything like your life today? How many times have we, like Old Testament Jacob, been going about our routine and suddenly realized, "The LORD is in this place, and I was not aware of it" (Genesis 28:16 NIV)?

. . . .

*Dear Papa God, please help me
to quiet down and listen for You. Amen.*

CREATIVE CONNECTION

But Jesus would often go to some
place where he could be alone and pray.

LUKE 5:16 CEV

Jesus is our best example of the importance—especially in the midst of our chaotic schedules—of finding a quiet place to listen for the Father's voice. Christ often slipped away from the clamoring crowds to find an isolated place to pray, devoid of distractions.

One of my favorite places to commune with the Lord is in my car. I call it my rolling cathedral. The prayer list in my glove compartment and praise music bouncing off the ceiling liner keep me spiritually uplifted while my eyes are earthbound. And it's a good time to listen—really listen—for that still, small voice while I'm insulated from everyday noise and clutter.

. . . .

Dear Papa God, please help me to get creative in
finding quiet times to connect with You. Amen.

STEAL AWAY AND PRAY

*Submit yourselves, then, to God. Resist the devil,
and he will flee from you. Come near to God
and he will come near to you.*

JAMES 4:7–8 NIV

When my kids were little, my "prayer closet" was literally just that. I'd lock myself in my walk-in closet as the kids wiggled their fingers beneath the door. "Shoo!" I'd say. "This is Mommy's special God time." Bible in hand, I'd curl up beside my shoes and feel my spirit rejuvenate through ten precious minutes of alone time with the Lover of my soul. Today I steal away to a secluded hammock in my backyard or take a prayer walk. If I'm really feeling depleted, I'll bolt for a retreat.

What's your favorite place to steal away and pray?

. . . .

*Dear Papa God, I want regular, uninterrupted
times to come near to You and have You
come near to me. Please help me to discipline
myself to carve out these times. Amen.*

HOW TO PRAY

You should pray like this: Our Father in heaven, help us to honor your name. Come and set up your kingdom, so that everyone on earth will obey you, as you are obeyed in heaven. Give us our food for today. Forgive us for doing wrong, as we forgive others. Keep us from being tempted and protect us from evil.

MATTHEW 6:9–13 CEV

Some people, especially new believers, feel uncomfortable praying because they aren't sure how to approach the omnipotent Creator of all things. And if you're not used to it, it can feel intimidating to pour out your heart to someone you can't see (although we women seem to have no problem with that on a telephone!).

So how should we pray? Our example, the Lord's Prayer, was given by Jesus in Matthew 6:9–13 and Luke 11:2–4.

. . . .

Dear Papa God, please help me not to be intimidated by coming to You in prayer. You know and love me better than anyone. Help me to learn how to pray from Your Word. Amen.

THE BEST KIND OF FRUIT

*"By their fruit you will recognize them.
Do people pick grapes from thornbushes,
or figs from thistles? Likewise, every good tree
bears good fruit, but a bad tree bears bad fruit."*
MATTHEW 7:16–17 NIV

Galatians 5:22–23 (NLT) says, "The Holy Spirit produces this kind of fruit in our lives: love, joy, peace, patience, kindness, goodness, faithfulness, gentleness, and self-control." I think it's interesting that the first four fruits are internal; they're a result of the Holy Spirit's presence altering our attitudes. Like holy underwear, they support us where it counts and beautify us from the foundation up. The last five are external, the visible proof that God's Spirit within us is vibrant and thriving.

. . . .

Dear Papa God, I want people to know me by my fruit, the kind of fruit that comes from Your Holy Spirit. Please help love, joy, peace, patience, kindness, goodness, faithfulness, gentleness, and self-control to grow abundantly in my life. Amen.

JOY OF THE LORD = STRENGTH

Nehemiah said, "Go and enjoy choice food and sweet drinks, and send some to those who have nothing prepared. This day is holy to our Lord. Do not grieve, for the joy of the LORD is your strength."
NEHEMIAH 8:10 NIV

Some time ago, I made the conscious decision to be someone who seeks joy, regardless of her circumstances. It hasn't been easy. But I've come to see that joy is a commitment we make, even more important than commitments like choosing a marriage partner, or political party, or profession, or church. Joy is not just an emotion but a way of life. Not a reaction but a transaction. It's signing on the dotted line that we believe: Security is not our god. Good health is not our god. Happiness is not our god. God is our God.

And He promises that His joy is our very strength (Nehemiah 8:10).

• •

Dear Papa God, I want to seek and choose the joy that comes from You in any and all circumstances. You are my God and my strength. Amen.

JOY TRUMPS HAPPINESS

Rejoice always.
1 THESSALONIANS 5:16 NKJV

Always be joyful—how is that possible? Are we supposed to just naively turn our backs on all the bad things that happen? Hang up on bill collectors? Ignore that breast lump? Avoid marriage counseling when our home is a conversation graveyard?

Of course not.

The problem is that we often confuse happiness with joy. Happiness is directly related to our external situation—hey, there's enough money in the bank to pay the bills this month! Are these pants actually looser? Hooray!

But joy comes from a deeper level. The it-is-well-with-my-soul level; the bottom-of-my-heart place where we trust the Lord enough to not only believe but actually behave like He is sovereign and whatever happens to us is part of His plan.

Dear Papa God, true joy from You totally trumps happiness. Please fill me with Your joy and help me to share it with others. Amen.

SUPERNATURAL JOY

You make known to me the path of life; you will
fill me with joy in your presence, with eternal
pleasures at your right hand.
PSALM 16:11 NIV

My pastor, Mark Saunders, says, "Happy sometimes doesn't come in the Christ-following package, but joy always does."

We just have to rip off the paper and unwrap the package.

Experiencing joy in the throes of hard times is something that can't be explained, really—it's purely supernatural. It's one of the amazing mysteries of our faith. But I can attest that it's real: When we sincerely ask the Holy Spirit to fill us with the joy of the Lord and commit to focus on that joy, He'll do it. We're suddenly, amazingly, miraculously overflowing with His warmth and love and hope.

· ·

Dear Papa God, you don't promise me
happiness, which is based on circumstances.
You promise me joy that surpasses
circumstances in a supernatural way. That's
amazing, and I thank You and praise You! Amen.

CALM IN THE STORM

And he arose, and rebuked the wind, and said unto the sea, Peace, be still. And the wind ceased, and there was a great calm.

MARK 4:39 KJV

"Peace, be still." Wow. Three simple words calmed the winds, stilled the storm, and brought peace to those in turmoil. Just what we hope Jesus will do to the storms in our lives. No more retching over the rails, no more floundering about while forces over which you have no control hurl you to and fro.

Hey, did you notice where Jesus was during the worst of the tempest? He was in the stern, curled up on a pillow, asleep. Does that sound like someone panicking about his horrendous situation?

Not at all. It sounds like someone who knew the outcome of the storm all along. Someone at complete peace with God and Himself, regardless of His circumstances. Someone whom I aspire to emulate.

. . . .

Dear Papa God, I have no need to panic in the storms of life because You are always more powerful and You give supernatural peace. Still, it's hard to remain calm. Please help me. Amen.

CALM IN OUR HEARTS

May the Lord of peace himself give you peace at all times and in every way. The Lord be with all of you.
2 THESSALONIANS 3:16 NIV

Jesus doesn't always quell the storms of our lives, does He? Sometimes we have to experience the strength of the wind and waves before we can appreciate the peace He brings. And it might not be external peace at all; our outward circumstances might continue to surge all around us, but that doesn't mean He can't bring us internal peace in the midst of the chaos. "The LORD gives strength to his people; the LORD blesses his people with peace" (Psalm 29:11 NIV).

Sometimes Jesus calms the storm, and sometimes He calms our hearts.

. . . .

Dear Papa God, help me to keep trusting You even while the storm rages on with no end in sight. Your sovereignty does not change in those times, and You can give me peace despite my circumstances. Thank You! Amen.

COMMIT WISELY

Be very careful, then, how you live—not as unwise but as wise, making the most of every opportunity, because the days are evil. Therefore do not be foolish, but understand what the Lord's will is.

EPHESIANS 5:15–17 NIV

It takes gumption to achieve a workable balance of your commitments, especially if you think you must meekly accept each and every project thrust your way. Cease and desist, girl! You don't have to do everything anybody asks you to do. You hereby have permission to say, "No!" God only sends specific responsibilities your way; the rest you add on your own. Discernment is crucial. Ask yourself: Is this task a wise use of my limited time and God-given talents and abilities, or will it only add confusion to my life and detract from what I should be doing?

. . . .

Dear Papa God, there are so many good ways to spend my time, but there is only so much time in a day! Please give me wisdom to choose the best things You want me to do and to be okay with saying no to the others. Amen.

GET BACK UP

We can make our plans,
but the Lᴏʀᴅ determines our steps.
Pʀᴏᴠᴇʀʙs 16:9 NLT

Remember when your little tyke discovered the fine art of equilibrium while learning to ride his bicycle? Concentration, lots of falls, and constant readjustment were necessary for him to finally find the right combination of factors that enabled him to remain upright and in control while careening down the driveway.

Balancing work, faith, and family takes the same kind of determination and focus. Sure, you'll make some mistakes, but after a fall you must pick yourself up, wipe the gravel off your skinned knees, and keep pedaling until you can remain upright and in control.

. . . .

Dear Papa God, I need balance in my schedule.
Please help me to prioritize my time and tasks
in a way that honors You. Amen.

BALANCE THE SEESAW

Whatever you say or do should be done in the name of the Lord Jesus, as you give thanks to God the Father because of him.

COLOSSIANS 3:17 CEV

The only hope we have for enduring past lunchtime tomorrow is to put God on one side of the seesaw and everything else on the other side. He's our balance! Then we're not slammed into the ground, nor are we left flailing in the air. At last we're on an even keel. When we achieve balance, our responsibilities no longer feel overwhelming. In fact, they feel not only manageable but fulfilling!

It's true that the storms of life can fling us about until we don't know which end is up. We may lose our equilibrium for a while, but we can learn, like the psalmist, to "embrace peace—don't let it get away!" (Psalm 34:14 MSG).

* *

Dear Papa God, whenever I feel off-kilter, please remind me that the answer to my balance problems is always You! Please guide and direct and stabilize me. Amen.

AN EXTRA DOLLOP

Patience and gentle talk can convince
a ruler and overcome any problem.
PROVERBS 25:15 CEV

I truly believe God gives mothers an extra dollop of patience, because if He didn't, we'd all be bald, twitching, and calling our lawyers from the slammer. When our kids are young, we learn to pack up our patience in a paper bag and take it with us wherever we go.

Patience. . .the plantain in the fruit basket of the spirit; a mature second cousin to peace (the banana). It's that elusive virtue we're afraid to ask God for more of, lest He give us more reason to need it.

* *

Dear Papa God, a mother sure needs extra doses of patience to be able to teach her kids through all sorts of mistakes and behavior issues while loving them in generous and wise ways. Please help! Amen.

NOT FOR WIMPS

Yet I am confident I will see the LORD's goodness while I am here in the land of the living. Wait patiently for the LORD. Be brave and courageous. Yes, wait patiently for the LORD.

PSALM 27:13–14 NLT

Patience certainly isn't for wimps. Take a closer look at Psalm 27:14. The psalmist links patience directly with courage; in other words, it takes a brave soul to employ the strength and fortitude necessary to be patient in the heat of difficult situations.

Patience is not passive; it's a dynamic, intentional process that grows with time, maturity, and insight. "A person's wisdom yields patience" (Proverbs 19:11 NIV).

* *

Dear Papa God, I struggle so much with waiting, especially when I'm praying for You to act in a situation and Your answer is repeatedly "Not yet." Please give me wise, courageous patience to keep on living for You with peace and joy, even in the wait times. Amen.

COURAGE WHILE WAITING

Let your hope make you glad. Be patient in time of trouble and never stop praying.
ROMANS 12:12 CEV

I so admire people who have the courage to be patient. To wait on the Lord's timing, even for something you want so badly it takes invasive bites out of your personal peace. When I feel that I've used up my daily patience quota, I often take the coward's way out and lash out in frustration. But there is no shelf life on patience.

Someone once said, "We may not all develop patience as quickly as we want, but we can learn to tolerate our impatience better."

That's my short-term goal: to tolerate my impatience better. I'm constantly learning and growing, but I've still got a long way to go to achieve real patience.

. . . .

Dear Papa God, please forgive me when I lash out in impatience. Help me to grow in courageous patience, trusting that Your timing is always best. Amen.

PATIENCE POINTS TO JESUS

*God is patient, because he wants everyone
to turn from sin and no one to be lost.*

2 PETER 3:9 CEV

What's your most recurring temper missile? What pushes your launch buttons? Do you have a countdown, or do you leap directly from "10, 9, 8" to blastoff?

As irritated as I get with myself and others and feel like I'm the most impatient person in the world, I find comfort in knowing the apostle Paul felt the same way about himself. "Since I was worse than anyone else, God had mercy on me and let me be an example of the endless patience of Christ Jesus. He did this so that others would put their faith in Christ and have eternal life" (1 Timothy 1:16 CEV).

My long-term goal is the same as Paul's: to point others to Christ Jesus. God's never-ending patience with me motivates me to develop patience with others so that they too can come to know His mercy and grace.

. . . .

*Dear Papa God, I desperately need, and I'm
desperately grateful for, Your patience with me
when I fail repeatedly. Help me to extend extreme
patience to others and point them to You. Amen.*

HEROES OF PATIENCE

*Learn to be patient, so that you will please God
and be given what he has promised.*
HEBREWS 10:36 CEV

Author Adel Bestavros said, "Patience with others is love; patience with self is hope; patience with God is faith." Just look at some of our biblical examples of faithful people waiting on the Lord's timing: Noah, waiting for rain as he toiled away on the ark month after month; Esther, waiting for years to find out how God would use her. And don't forget David, who, while waiting to grow up to be a warrior, found God using him as a boy to slay a giant and change the attitude of a nation.

Papa God wants to use us as examples of His patience too—yep, flawed ole you and me. Even as we're waiting to grow up (spiritually), you never know how He might use us today, despite mud puddles, or ant bites, or temper missiles.

· ·

*Dear Papa God, please help me to learn
from the heroes of faith and patience in Your
Word, waiting patiently on You to work in
my life the way You see fit. Amen.*

THE KIWI OF KINDNESS

"Love your enemies! Do good to them. Lend to them without expecting to be repaid. Then your reward from heaven will be very great, and you will truly be acting as children of the Most High, for he is kind to those who are unthankful and wicked. You must be compassionate, just as your Father is compassionate."

LUKE 6:35–36 NLT

In the fruit basket of the Spirit, kindness is the kiwi—the green smiley face in your compote. The wonderful virtue that compelled Jesus to heal the lame, return sight to the blind, feed the hungry, and give lepers their lives back. And He wants us to treat each other with the same kindness: "All of you, be like-minded, be sympathetic, love one another, be compassionate and humble" (1 Peter 3:8 NIV).

Easier said than done, isn't it? Especially in a modern world where kindness is often eyed with suspicion.

. . . .

Dear Papa God, in a world that's often skeptical of the motives behind kindness, help me to be kind anyway, showing compassion in a way that points people to You. Amen.

THE CANTALOUPE
OF GOODNESS

*Taste and see that the LORD is good;
blessed is the one who takes refuge in him.*
PSALM 34:8 NIV

Goodness is nothing from within ourselves but everything from God's orchestration. Goodness is not something we can manufacture by our own power but only channel from our heavenly Father. "No one is good but One, that is, God," Jesus reminded us in Matthew 19:17 (NKJV).

In the Spirit's fruit basket, goodness is the cantaloupe—sweet and juicy and bursting with the unique flavor of its Creator. God's flavor, His essence, is goodness. And the only way we can exude goodness in our lives is if He is dwelling within us.

. . . .

*Dear Papa God, You are good, always good!
Everything good in me and any goodness I give to
others comes directly from You. Thank You! Amen.*

THE STAR FRUIT OF FAITHFULNESS

For we live by faith, not by sight.
2 CORINTHIANS 5:7 NIV

Faithfulness is the Spirit's star fruit—symbolizing a glittering star for our crown in heaven. Faithfulness is the reward that starts giving during our days on earth and just keeps on giving for all eternity.

Faithfulness is really a kind of fruit salad made up of all the other fruits of the Spirit (love, joy, peace, patience, kindness, goodness, gentleness, and self-control). When all the fruits are mixed together in one bowl (person), a beautiful countenance and faithful lifestyle result. Like sweet ambrosia!

By definition, to be *faithful* is to "be steadfast in allegiance, to be loyal above all else"; in other words, acting out your relationship with the Lord. Physically demonstrating where your heart lies.

. . . .

Dear Papa God, I want my faith to be active,
not just something I say. Please help me to live out
my relationship with You for others to see so that
they'll want a relationship with You too. Amen.

THE MANGO OF GENTLENESS

But you, man of God, flee from all this,
and pursue righteousness, godliness, faith,
love, endurance and gentleness.

1 TIMOTHY 6:11 NIV

Gentleness is the delicate, fragrant mango in the fruit basket of the Spirit. There's no aroma quite like it. Gentleness is like a lovely scent that lingers behind us, a trace of God's exquisite fragrance in our own hearts that we leave in our wake, pointing others to Him.

We all know gentle, gracious people who do just that, don't we? Women whose intangible beauty glows from within. People who may not possess society's standards of physical attractiveness, but who leave us basking in their elegant beauty nonetheless.

• •

Dear Papa God, at times I feel like being harsh and blunt and loud, and it's hard to stay calm and tender. Please help me to develop more gentleness in my actions and reactions. Amen.

THE PRUNE OF SELF-CONTROL

Like a city whose walls are broken through
is a person who lacks self-control.
PROVERBS 25:28 NIV

Self-control is the prune of the Spirit; not the fruit you savor but the one vital for moving things along smoothly (if you've ever drunk prune juice, you know what I mean!). It's the fruit you gulp down and try not to choke on.

I think it's no coincidence that self-control is listed just behind gentleness in Galatians 5; they sprout from the same vine. You need to ingest the first in order to digest the second.

Self-control is courage fueled by integrity and supernatural power. It's something the average Jane doesn't have but is possessed only by those willing to step back from the firing line and hand over the lit match. "God's Spirit doesn't make cowards out of us. The Spirit gives us power, love, and self-control" (2 Timothy 1:7 CEV).

. . . .

Dear Papa God, I need such help with
self-control, whether it's in regard to avoiding
junk food or taming my tongue or watching my
attitude. The temptation to give in to my sin is
great, but Your Spirit is always greater. Amen.

UNLIKELY HERO

Then Joshua son of Nun secretly sent two spies from Shittim. "Go, look over the land," he said, "especially Jericho." So they went and entered the house of a prostitute named Rahab and stayed there.

JOSHUA 2:1 NIV

Rahab was the unlikeliest of heroes—a woman who sold her body to lusty men in dark shadows. Scum, we might say today. Yet she was the very person God chose to become a vital link in the lineage of King David and, later, Jesus Christ Himself. If a call girl can overcome her shady past and be extolled for her faithfulness, why can't we? Mother Teresa said, "Infinite possibilities are born of faith." Rahab is proof that God can—and will—use anyone with faith for His higher purposes. Anyone. How astoundingly freeing!

. . . .

Dear Papa God, at times I doubt what good I can possibly do for You to spread Your Gospel and share Your love. But please remind me that You are working in ways I cannot see, and You can use anyone willing to serve, even me. Amen.

IN THE DOWNTIMES

Love the Lᴏʀᴅ, all his faithful people! The Lᴏʀᴅ preserves those who are true to him, but the proud he pays back in full. Be strong and take heart, all you who hope in the Lᴏʀᴅ.
Psᴀʟᴍ 31:23–24 ɴɪᴠ

How do you remain faithful in the downtimes? The parched desert times when your faith shrivels and you feel all alone?

- *Seek God as your source. Seek Him first; He will give you the courage to be bold.*
- *Use your gifts, abilities, and, yes, disabilities to draw attention to Him.*
- *Spend time in His Word; feed your spirit daily.*
- *Reach out to others.*
- *Stay as beautiful as you can be, inside and outside. Never forget whom you represent.*
- *Talk yourself through difficulties. Literally tell yourself you can overcome any obstacle.*

Dear Papa God, when times are hard, help me be intentional in staying faithful to You. Amen.

SOUL SISTERS

You are better off to have a friend than to be all alone, because then you will get more enjoyment out of what you earn. If you fall, your friend can help you up. But if you fall without having a friend nearby, you are really in trouble.
ECCLESIASTES 4:9–10 CEV

Girlfriends. What would we do without 'em? They are the rare finds who hear the songs down deep in our souls and care enough to sing a duet when we can't manage a solo.

Everyone needs a soul sister, a kindred spirit who offers unconditional love and acceptance. Someone who believes we can be beautiful and overlooks our inner beast when it takes a bite out of her booty. A safe place where we can store our secrets and be sure they won't leak. Aristotle said, "The antidote for fifty enemies is one friend."

. . . .

Dear Papa God, the good friendships in my life are such an encouragement. I thank You for them! Amen.

DEALING WITH ANGER

A man's discretion makes him slow to anger,
and it is his glory to overlook a transgression.
PROVERBS 19:11 NASB

Did you know that it's not wrong to be angry? Nope, not according to Ephesians 4:26–27 (MSG): "Go ahead and be angry. You do well to be angry—but don't use your anger as fuel for revenge. And don't stay angry. Don't go to bed angry. Don't give the Devil that kind of foothold in your life."

Our God is a passionate God—He feels things. And He feels them strongly. We are made in His image, so we must never deny our feelings. We were created to feel. But after we feel passionate emotions, we need to bring those emotions under Christ's authority and then react accordingly.

. . . .

Dear Papa God, I need to remember that the anger I feel is not necessarily the problem; it's the way I react to it. Please help me give my anger to You. Amen.

NOT SO SWEET

Never pay back evil with more evil. . . . Dear friends, never take revenge. Leave that to the righteous anger of God. For the Scriptures say, "I will take revenge; I will pay them back," says the LORD.
ROMANS 12:17, 19 NLT

We all know the saying "Revenge is sweet," right? God actually has a different take on revenge.

"What? We shouldn't seek revenge?" we cry in outrage. "C'mon—it's only fair! What else can possibly satisfy that burning desire for justice in the depths of our being?"

Forgiveness. Yes ma'am, that's right.

But forgiveness doesn't come naturally in our revenge-glorified world. Because forgiveness is often impossible without the Holy Spirit's intervention, we feed off the power of one-upping someone who has wronged us. Forgiving others and accepting forgiveness are unique qualities in today's society.

. . . .

Dear Papa God, getting revenge on my own is so tempting, but please help me leave the wrongs done to me in Your care, to be dealt with by Your goodness and justice. Amen.

SLIPCOVER FOR THE SOUL

If we confess our sins, He is faithful and righteous to forgive us our sins and to cleanse us from all unrighteousness.

1 JOHN 1:9 NASB

Forgiveness is the slipcover for the soul. We're not defined by our mistakes; we're recovered and remodeled by forgiveness. We're made new and perky and beautiful! No one need ever remember the ugliness underneath—God guarantees us that He won't! "As far as the east is from the west, so far has he removed our transgressions from us" (Psalm 103:12 NIV).

So what do you think, sister? Does the stained couch of your life need a jazzy new slipcover? I hear the Divine Forgiveness Boutique is running a special!

. . . .

Dear Papa God, there aren't enough words in all the world to express my gratefulness for Your forgiveness of my sins, the way You remove them so far from me and cleanse me again and again. Thank You! Amen.

NOT ON A CURVE

For by grace you have been saved through faith;
and that not of yourselves, it is the gift of God;
not as a result of works, so that no one may boast.
EPHESIANS 2:8–9 NASB

Eligibility for entrance into heaven isn't graded on a curve; we don't get there by being better than someone else. We get there by faith alone. . .in Christ alone. . . by grace alone.

"Even before he made the world, God loved us and chose us in Christ to be holy and without fault in his eyes. God decided in advance to adopt us into his own family by bringing us to himself through Jesus Christ. This is what he wanted to do, and it gave him great pleasure" (Ephesians 1:4–5 NLT).

If we receive His precious gift of salvation, we don't have to fear death, dear friend. It's merely a door opening to the greatest adventure of all: heaven!

* *

Dear Papa God, thank You for Your precious
gift of salvation, available to all people,
not based on anything we could possibly do
but based on Your great love for us. Amen.

ENTHRALLED

Let the king be enthralled by your beauty;
honor him, for he is your lord.

PSALM 45:11 NIV

People love makeovers, but God loves transformations.

And once the transformation process has begun, He wants us to see ourselves as beautiful, as the same way He sees us. In fact, according to the scripture above, He will be enthralled by our beauty! Enthralled! That means charmed, captivated, spellbound. Whoa—who else in this whole wide world can we say is so absolutely smitten with us?

All the time we spend looking in the mirror, primping, adjusting, and reinventing ourselves, will be for naught if we're not beautified from the inside out. If that hideous beast within is not dealt with, it will emerge during times of emotional crisis and destroy everything good, everything lovely, everything beautiful in our lives with its vicious, relentless claws.

But Papa God equips us not only to fight the beast but also to subdue it permanently.

. . . .

Dear Papa God, I don't want merely a makeover.
I want Your transforming power in my life to give
me a beauty that is enthralling to You and
attracts others to You. Amen.

STRESS OVERLOAD

If you are tired from carrying heavy burdens, come to me and I will give you rest. Take the yoke I give you. Put it on your shoulders and learn from me. I am gentle and humble, and you will find rest. This yoke is easy to bear, and this burden is light.

MATTHEW 11:28–30 CEV

Stress overload symptoms don't appear overnight. If we ignore the signs, stress will eventually take a toll on our bodies.

We women tend to internalize stress. We take confrontation and subtle discord very personally. Heated words and even mild disagreements often sink into our innards, depositing a sense of unsettledness and anxiety. When we can't find an outlet for our pent-up frustration, we sometimes resort to self-destructive behavior. We eat too much. We smoke. We drink. We abuse our bodies. We may even isolate ourselves.

* *

Dear Papa God, please help me not to ignore the signs that I'm overdoing it in life. Help me to put You first, prioritize wisely, and bask in the peace and rest that will result. Amen.

ON CLEANING UP

*The Master said, "Martha, dear Martha,
you're fussing far too much and getting
yourself worked up over nothing. One thing
only is essential, and Mary has chosen it—it's
the main course, and won't be taken from her."*
LUKE 10:41–42 MSG

I try to clean up, but sometimes my efforts backfire. Like the Florida woman who accidentally hit an alligator with her car. Seriously. She dutifully cleaned up the road but crashed into a parked car when the possum-playing gator began thrashing around in her backseat. The poor dear was charged with felony possession of an alligator. (We can't count votes down here, but we're sure on top of illegal reptiles!)

So when we're tempted to forsake our time with Papa God, let's remember Jesus' words: "Dear Martha, you're fussing far too much and getting yourself worked up over nothing" (Luke 10:41 MSG).

Only one thing is truly of eternal importance: Papa God. And He created dirt.

. . . .

*Dear Papa God, please help me to find the wise
balance of keeping my home clean and organized
without stressing too much over it. Thank You! Amen.*

WHAT ARE YOU TELLING YOURSELF?

*Carefully guard your thoughts
because they are the source of true life.*
PROVERBS 4:23 CEV

Positive self-talk isn't just crucial in sports; it's a huge part of everyday stress management. When we tell ourselves something over and over, we eventually buy into it, and it becomes a part of our inner makeup, our self-esteem, our performance motivation—for better or worse. In essence, we choose our attitude, and that attitude dictates our stress level.

"Okay, that first soufflé flopped, but so did Julia Child's. I'll make a few adjustments and the next one will be the chef d'oeuvre." When we choose an upbeat attitude, our outlook becomes much more optimistic and consequently less stress-producing.

* *

*Dear Papa God, You created me in Your image
and love me unconditionally. Please help me
not to insult You by talking to myself negatively.
Help me to build myself up with loving,
encouraging truth from Your Word. Amen.*

STOP CHANNELING EEYORE

You'll do best by filling your minds and meditating on things true, noble, reputable, authentic, compelling, gracious—the best, not the worst; the beautiful, not the ugly; things to praise, not things to curse. Put into practice what you learned from me, what you heard and saw and realized. Do that, and God, who makes everything work together, will work you into his most excellent harmonies.

PHILIPPIANS 4:8–9 MSG

Channeling Eeyore becomes the soundtrack for our subconscious thoughts. Those mopey, self-deprecating thoughts wear us down and wear us out. We're actually sabotaging ourselves. We settle for defeat when, with a few minor attitude adjustments, we could open the door to amazing possibilities.

The worst part of negative self-talk is that we're not only limiting ourselves; we're also limiting God. The Creator of the universe. The One who is ready to fill us with expectancy, hope, and potential, and wants us instead to tell ourselves, "I can do everything through Christ, who gives me strength" (Philippians 4:13 NLT).

. . . .

Dear Papa God, how can I possibly think negatively if I keep my mind on You? Amen.

MODERATION

*Let God transform you into a new person by changing
the way you think. Then you will learn to know God's
will for you, which is good and pleasing and perfect.*

ROMANS 12:2 NLT

Are you overextending yourself? Spreading your time or
energies too thin? Regardless of how well-intentioned
we are, we're only human. The Master Designer, who
created us and knows our limitations, wants us to set
parameters, to pick and choose the way we expend
our finite energies.

To shove the envelope not only robs our joy and
ability to live in the moment, but also steals fulfill-
ment and effectiveness from the priorities God has
appointed as our primary focus for this particular season
of our life. Ben Franklin said it well with this advice:
"Do every- thing in moderation, including moderation."

. . . .

*Dear Papa God, it's so difficult to choose
the best things to do with my time. Please help
me to do things in moderation, always taking
time to rest and rejuvenate in order to know
Your perfect will for me. Amen.*

HE NEVER LETS YOU DOWN

He has never let you down, never looked the other way when you were being kicked around. . .he has been right there, listening.
PSALM 22:24 MSG

It's easy to question God's love for us and even His very existence when tragedy strikes. And in our fallen world, it will strike everyone at one time or another. My husband, Chuck, and I both went through our own barren desert times in our faith after six heart-wrenching miscarriages. In the immediate throes of our loss, God seemed cruel and heartless. We felt abandoned and lost, but in retrospect, we now see that God was still there all along. Not cruel, not heartless, just silently shining a flashlight of hope and waiting patiently for our self-imposed spiritual cataracts to slough off so we could see His presence.

One of my favorite scriptures of comfort became Psalm 22:24. I came to understand that God is not our afflictor; no, He's the helper of the afflicted. That's you and me. He's not the enemy; He's on our team. A huge difference to a healing heart!

. . . .

Dear Papa God, please help me to run to You when I'm hurting and doubting, never away from You. Amen.

PULLED AND STRETCHED

No discipline is enjoyable while it is happening—it's painful! But afterward there will be a peaceful harvest of right living for those who are trained in this way.

HEBREWS 12:11 NLT

Have you ever baked homemade bread? Nothing smells better this side of heaven! Well, the way I see it, the process of healing is like bread yeast—the dough has to be pulled, stretched, and beat upon to work the yeast throughout, but it finally permeates every inch. Over time, that very yeast enables the bread to rise and become what it was meant to be. If the yeast doesn't pervade the dough, or if the loaf doesn't spend enough time in the oven, the bread will never be completed. It will remain useless, gloppy, inedible dough. Heat is necessary for its transformation and perfection.

So the next time you feel like yelling, "Stick a toothpick in me; I'm done!" remember that although our oven days are difficult—often painful—those are the times we grow and mature in our faith.

. . . .

Dear Papa God, please give me perspective of how discipline can teach me, change me, and draw me closer to You. Amen.

TIME FOR A BREATHER

Make it your goal to live a quiet life.
1 THESSALONIANS 4:11 NLT

Remember how it felt to wake up on a gloriously free summer morning when you were a kid? Ah, the exultation of knowing you had empty hours to fill any way you liked!

As adults, we don't often have the luxury of having free hours, but we can carve free minutes out of each day if we diligently simplify and unclog those constipated calendars. That, dear sister, is when we reconnect with that summer morning feeling. The joy of the Lord brings splashes of color back into our black-and-white world.

. . . .

Dear Papa God, please help me to carve out time every day for a breather that glorifies You and lets me appreciate the joy You put into my life. Amen.

OTHERS FIRST

Don't be selfish; don't try to impress others. Be humble, thinking of others as better than yourselves. Don't look out only for your own interests, but take an interest in others, too.

PHILIPPIANS 2:3–4 NLT

Submitting to others boils down to a matter of trust that the Lord is in ultimate control.

When we choose to submit to someone in authority over us, we're actually submitting to God. If He truly is in control, He orchestrates the channels of authority in which we live, work, and function. As believers, our ultimate goal is to become Christlike, and Christ exemplified willing submission to His Father by humbling Himself even to the point of death.

May "As you wish" be our love-motivated creed too, as we submit to Philippians 2:3 and humble ourselves to the point of viewing others as more important than ourselves.

. . . .

Dear Papa God, it's often hard to submit to others and not think of myself as most important. Please help me to be humble and respectful of others, especially those in authority over me. Amen.

CHRONIC WORRY

Cast your cares on the LORD and he will sustain you;
he will never let the righteous be shaken.
PSALM 55:22 NIV

When we worry chronically, we don't see what's really happening; truth is obscured by lies we choose to believe. It's okay. Everything's fine. Sure, I'm exhausted and miserable right now, but it'll be better next week. Next month. Next year.

Sister, it's time to do something about being a worry slave today.

How can we turn off that oppressive fret faucet? The first step is to give your worries to Jesus. When your hands start wringing or the mental obsession recorder hits REPLAY for the tenth time, lay your problems at the foot of the cross. Jesus will take them off your hands. Repeat this process every time you try to wrestle them back.

. . . .

Dear Papa God, You are so good to want to take
my worries and anxiety and burdens away from me!
Why do I ever think I should hold on to them? Please
help me release and trust them to You. Amen.

HUMOR IN HARD TIMES

"He will once again fill your mouth with laughter and your lips with shouts of joy."

JOB 8:21 NLT

Humor is important. It's a catalyst for releasing God's rejuvenating joy into our souls. Humor is God's weapon against worry, anxiety, and fear. It's a powerful salve for the skinned knees of the spirit. . .healing, revitalizing, protecting us against toxic infections like bitterness, defeat, or depression.

Laughter is our lifeline when we're sinking into the pit of rigidity, when we're so absorbed in the stressful details of our lives that we're missing the fun. The sun hasn't disappeared just because it's temporarily obscured by clouds. Sometimes those silver linings are just a belly laugh away.

. . . .

Dear Papa God, even during hard times, please help me to keep a good sense of humor. Amen.

SWALLOW THAT PRIDE

*And whatever you do or say, do it as
a representative of the Lord Jesus, giving
thanks through him to God the Father.*
COLOSSIANS 3:17 NLT

Pride is an underhanded thief. It sneaks up and robs us of the heart-changing gratitude that is a by-product of knowing—and acknowledging—that our attributes, abilities, and accolades are simply gifts from our Creator. Gifts wrapped in love and tied with a bow of grace.

My friend Rich, a teacher and father, has an infectious attitude of humility. When teachers at the Christian school where he worked were told that budget cuts necessitated that staff assume janitorial duties, grumbling broke out among the ranks. During the protests and discussion that ensued, Rich quietly disappeared with the cleaning supplies. When discovered scrubbing toilets on his knees, Rich replied, "Kneeling at this throne is no different than kneeling at God's throne—it's all for His glory!"

* *

*Dear Papa God, may I never be too prideful to
do anything You ask me to do. Help me to serve
others and do all things for Your glory. Amen.*

SHACKLED BY PERFECTIONISM?

Don't waste your time on useless work, mere busywork, the barren pursuits of darkness.
EPHESIANS 5:16 MSG

How can we grand dames of disarray cope with the ravages of anarchic untidiness and keep our stress thermometers from erupting like Mount Vesuvius?

I've discovered the key: we must lower our expectations. That's right, pitch the perfectionism, lose the legalism, cast off comparisons. Limbo under that self-imposed bar of spotlessness. We're not in competition for the cleanest house award. Who cares if the gal next door's showerhead is shinier than yours?

I'm not saying we should wallow in pigsties, but when we're shackled by perfectionism, we become slaves to our homes. They own us instead of us owning them. Not good. Not wise. Not pleasing to God.

God wants us to invest our precious minutes on earth in people not things. Focus on pursuing those whose souls hang in the balance of eternity.

* *

Dear Papa God, help me not to be a slave to my home or an over-perfectionist. How I maintain relationships is more important than how I maintain my home; I just need a balance of the two. Amen.

NEW MERCIES
EVERY MORNING

The Lord's kindness never fails! If he had not been merciful, we would have been destroyed. The Lord can always be trusted to show mercy each morning.
LAMENTATIONS 3:22–23 CEV

While fleeing willy-nilly from God, Jonah's poor decisions resulted in his being ingested by a monstrous water-dwelling creature. Without God's intervention, he would have ended up a seafood appetizer.

Jehovah chose to overlook Jonah's hardheaded disobedience and rescue his bony behind anyway. That, girlfriend, is mercy.

And what about me? What about you? We're no different than Jonah. We too run away from difficult places or daunting tasks or annoying people God has placed in our lives. The same questions apply: Why does God care about stubborn, rebellious creatures? Why should He waste His time rescuing hapless victims of their own bad choices? We certainly don't deserve His mercy.

Yet He lovingly extends it to us anyway. Over and over and over again.

. . . .

Dear Papa God, Your Word says Your mercies are new every morning. Thank You for Your unending faithfulness to me. Amen.

REJUVENATE

And people should eat and drink and enjoy the fruits of their labor, for these are gifts from God.
ECCLESIASTES 3:13 NLT

Studies show that there are definite correlations between enjoyable activities and stress reduction. In fact, stress management professionals recommend that you engage in at least one activity weekly just for fun. But hey, why stop at one?

Not only are fun activities a key stress-coping mechanism, but cultivating relaxing hobbies provides a way to express yourself, sharpen latent talents (or develop skills you always wished you had), and release pent-up angst. We may not be able to eliminate stress from our crazy lives, but we can empower ourselves to weather the stress better by pursuing rejuvenating activities that refill our joy tanks rather than suck us bone dry.

. . . .

Dear Papa God, sometimes I forget to just take time to relax and enjoy the beautiful world You've created and the creativity You've placed in me. Please help me to find activities that help me rest and rejuvenate. Amen.

ABUNDANT, FUN LIFE

*"The thief's purpose is to steal and kill and destroy.
My purpose is to give them a rich and satisfying life."*
JOHN 10:10 NLT

About now you're probably thinking, I shouldn't be wasting time doing fun things for myself. I have my family to take care of. C'mon, now, shed the guilt, sister—fun is good for you and your family members! You're investing in your health and future, which directly affect their health and futures as well.

Scientists have proven that laughter increases circulation and exercises skeletal muscles (unfortunately, that includes sphincter muscles if you laugh too hard!). One study I read about confirmed that laughing fifteen minutes every morning for three weeks significantly increased optimism, positive emotions, social identification, and. . .um, regulation.

Bye-bye, prune juice.

Fun is actually contagious! A British medical journal concluded from social experiments that happiness transferred between people can last up to a year. A year! When you smile, the whole world really does smile with you!

. . . .

*Dear Papa God, living for You doesn't mean
a somber, legalistic, religious-ritual-filled life,
but an abundant, fun life of hope, peace,
and great joy. Thank You! Amen.*

WINNING THE PRIZE!

*How can a believer be a
partner with an unbeliever?*
2 CORINTHIANS 6:15 NLT

What's wrong with being choosy in our relationships? Isn't that the underlying message of 2 Corinthians 6:15? Shared faith is often the glue that holds a dry and shriveling relationship together until it can be reconditioned. Our Lord specializes in repairing rips in relationships. He's more than happy to provide the marital cord strength when two of the strands become frayed: "A cord of three strands is not quickly torn apart" (Ecclesiastes 4:12 NASB).

Yes, romance is based on a lot more than wine and roses. Or soda and wieners, for that matter. I once heard a man introduce his spouse as "my trophy wife." When asked why he used that term, he looked adoringly at his wife and replied with a big smile, "Because I won the prize!" What a wonderful way for a man to view love!

. . . .

*Dear Papa God, thank You for my husband.
May our marriage, while not perfect,
display Your love. Amen.*

TRUE LOVE

Show love in everything you do.
1 Corinthians 16:14 CEV

According to 1 Corinthians 13:4–6 (CEV), true romantic love is rooted in the unconditional acceptance God demonstrates toward us: "Love is kind and patient, never jealous, boastful, proud, or rude. Love isn't selfish or quick tempered. It doesn't keep a record of wrongs that others do. Love rejoices in the truth, but not in evil."

Wow! What a list of romance-enhancers! Imagine the potential of a relationship where both partners are kind and patient with one another, never rude or pouty or resentful. A true partnership where hurt feelings don't compound and previous mistakes are totally forgiven and forgotten. Where truth is the norm and transparency is not risky.

. . . .

Dear Papa God, thank You for the
wisdom in Your Word on which
to build a lasting marriage. Amen.

DEALING WITH THE DIFFICULT

"If your enemies are hungry, give them something to eat. And if they are thirsty, give them something to drink. This will be the same as piling burning coals on their heads." Don't let evil defeat you, but defeat evil with good.
Romans 12:20–21 cev

Unresolved conflict can definitely increase our feelings of anxiety and tension, which escalate over time. Like scum building up in the corners of the shower, emotional residue can dirty the edges of our peace without our even realizing it. As unsettling as it can be at the moment, it's important to deal with situations as they arise and not carry them around for weeks or even years like stinky loaded diapers.

Difficult people often are in our lives for unseen purposes. God's purposes. Perhaps to stretch us, grow us, or sand down our sharp edges by their friction.

. . . .

Dear Papa God, I desperately need Your help to deal with difficult people in a way that pleases You. Please help me to see them through Your eyes, with Your love. Amen.

PARENTAL ENGAGEMENT

*"But as for me and my household,
we will serve the LORD."*
JOSHUA 24:15 NIV

Worrying about negative influences on our children is a leading stress-producer for women, but it's such a relief to know there's something we can do about it.

A Columbia University study showed that teens who eat with their families five or more times weekly are less likely to smoke, drink, and hang out with sexually active friends. Joseph A. Califano Jr., chairman and president of the National Center on Addiction and Substance Abuse, puts it best: "Parental engagement is a critical weapon in the fight against substance abuse. If I could wave a wand, I'd make everyone have family dinners."

My synopsis? The family that chews together stays glued together.

* *

Dear Papa God, You love my kids even more than I do. Please give me the wisdom and love I need to connect with them well and point them to You. May Your love keep our family glued together. Amen.

A LASTING FAITH DYNASTY

*Every day I will praise you and extol your name
for ever and ever. Great is the L<small>ORD</small> and most
worthy of praise; his greatness no one can fathom.
One generation commends your works to another;
they tell of your mighty acts.*
P<small>SALM</small> 145:2–4 NIV

We pass on bits and pieces of ourselves to our children;
these morsels, in turn, are passed on to countless future
generations. We can't help the flat feet and connect-
the-dots freckles they inherit, but we can intentionally
transfer specific character-molding traits: dependency
on God, the habit of prayer, loyalty, integrity, and love
for and protection of each other within the family.

The key is to ask ourselves: Am I living my faith
out loud? Am I making it a priority to ensure that my
legacy includes a living, breathing, dynamic relationship
with my heavenly Father? It's never too late to lay the
foundation for a strong and lasting faith dynasty!

. . . .

*Dear Papa God, I want to live out an authentic
relationship with You for my kids to see every day,
that they might desire such a relationship too and
someday their children and so on. Amen.*

A LIFESTYLE OF GRATITUDE

Give thanks in all circumstances.
1 THESSALONIANS 5:18 NIV

I just read about university research concluding that those who are grateful on a regular basis are healthier mentally and physically. It's like going to the gym—you can't go just once a year and expect to benefit; you've got to make it a habit. Living gratefully doesn't come naturally—it's a discipline we have to consider important enough to adopt. Like having a daily quiet time or flossing our teeth.

I find it amazing that studies actually prove thankful people are less envious and resentful. Grateful people sleep better, are physically more active, and have lower blood pressure. Guess I could stand a little more of that, huh, Lord? There are perks to a lifestyle of gratitude.

. . . .

Dear Papa God, You are so good to me, and I don't thank You enough. Help me to see and count my blessings daily for a lifestyle of gratitude. Amen.

THE GARDEN OF FRIENDSHIP

*You are better off to have a friend than to be all
alone, because then you will get more enjoyment
out of what you earn. If you fall, your friend can
help you up. But if you fall without having a
friend nearby, you are really in trouble.*
ECCLESIASTES 4:9–10 CEV

Have you ever seen an overgrown garden? A once beautiful, well-tended, manicured landscape that has grown unkempt and ugly? The lovely place that once lit eyes with gladness begins to turn them away in repulsion. All because of inattention. Lack of investment. Indifference.

So how do we find time to nurture friendships so they don't become like neglected gardens? To be the friend that our friend needs?

- *Make girlfriend time a priority.*
- *Do life together.*
- *Grow together.*
- *Let her know you're praying for her often.*
- *Celebrate together. For anything and everything.*
- *Hold hands through the tough times.*

*Dear Papa God, please bless me with good girlfriends
and help me to be a good friend too. Amen.*

JUST TO SHOW YOU CARE

*We should keep on encouraging each other
to be thoughtful and to do helpful things.*
HEBREWS 10:24 CEV

I will never forget how my girlfriend Cheryl ministered to me when I was sidelined by a skiing accident that required three surgeries on my left knee within seven months. Cheryl tuned in to my depressed spirit carefully tucked beneath a smiling exterior. Every second or third day, month after month, I received a three-minute phone call simply inquiring, "How are you today?"

Some days I burst into tears when I heard her voice; other days we chatted about inane life happenings. But always, her faithful, assuring "Just wanted you to know I was thinking about you" healed me more thoroughly than any medical treatment ever could.

. . . .

*Dear Papa God, help me to realize it doesn't
take much, even just a quick phone call, to let
someone know how much I care. Help me to
be a good friend and encourager. Amen.*

LOVING OUR SIBLINGS

Be kind and merciful, and forgive others,
just as God forgave you because of Christ.
EPHESIANS 4:32 CEV

Siblings are the reluctant instructors in our life classrooms. They're our crash dummies, our failed experiments, the unfortunate people we practice on to learn how not to treat others. They unwittingly teach us civility by being the ones who suffer the consequences of our mistakes as we learn the virtues of kindness, compassion, fairness, forgiveness, and helping one another.

Yet despite trampled feelings, bruises, and occasional concussions, there are no more loyal companions than siblings. We're roses and tulips from the same garden! What would we do without them? They're as much a part of our DNA as our crooked noses. We love them, admire them, and are irritated senseless by them all at the same time.

. . . .

Dear Papa God, my siblings are a blessing, even
when we don't see eye to eye. Thank You for them,
and help me to love and encourage them. Amen.

TWO HUSBANDS

*Wives should always put their husbands first,
as the church puts Christ first. A husband
should love his wife as much as Christ loved
the church and gave his life for it.*

EPHESIANS 5:24–25 CEV

I try to remember that I really have two husbands: Chuck and Jesus. As a believer, part of the bride of Christ, I am married to Him as well (see Ephesians 5:25–27; Revelation 21:9). Ishi, the Hebrew name for God used in Hosea 2:16, is translated as "husband." The Lover of our soul assumes the traditional husband's role as protector, provider, and faithful companion. Only He will never leave us or forsake us—He refuses to divorce us no matter how unfaithful we are.

What a revelation when we view our wifely role through that perspective! We begin to see our mates through the same compassionate, forgiving, unconditionally loving eyes with which Christ sees us. Our husband's desires become important to us. We want to meet his needs.

* *

Dear Papa God, thank You that You are the Lover of my soul who will never let me down. My earthly husband might, but I love him dearly anyway, and I want our marriage to reflect Your grace and love. Amen.

THE BEST KIND OF GIFT

Children are a gift from the LORD;
they are a reward from him.

PSALM 127:3 NLT

My best motherhood stress reliever has been to remind myself in the midst of the fray that the most important things in my world are my people. My peeps. Those beautiful souls God has entrusted to my care for a few short years. They require and deserve the best of my attention even as my day is constantly interrupted by their blessings.

"Don't you see that children are GOD's best gift?" (Psalm 127:3 MSG). Did you catch that, fellow frazzled mom? God's very best gift is our children.

If we can just keep grasping that elusive reassurance even as our groping fingernails cling to the last shreds of maternal sanity, we'll be okay.

. . . .

Dear Papa God, even on the hardest parenting
days, remind me moment by moment what a gift
my children are. I thank You for them, and I beg
You for wisdom and patience as I parent them. Amen.

TEMPLE CARETAKERS

*Don't you realize that your body is the temple
of the Holy Spirit, who lives in you and was
given to you by God? You do not belong to
yourself, for God bought you with a high price.
So you must honor God with your body.*
1 CORINTHIANS 6:19–20 NLT

One of the most important and long-lasting relationships we must cultivate is with these earth suits God has entrusted to us for a limited time. Depending on the condition in which we maintain them, our bodies can be warmly comforting, a source of pleasure, a vehicle for adventure, or a painfully restrictive straitjacket.

The Bible says our bodies are God's temples. If we, as temple caretakers, are to withstand battering gales and the onslaught of relentless enemy attacks, we must fortify our living structures from within! Knowledge and prevention of the forces assaulting our temple edifices are our best defense.

• •

*Dear Papa God, please help me to do a better job
of treating my body as Your temple. I need healthy
habits and a smart balance of not stressing about
my body but taking good care of it. Amen.*

DON'T DESPAIR

*"Don't despair. Your GOD is present among you,
a strong Warrior there to save you. Happy to
have you back, he'll calm you with his love
and delight you with his songs."*
ZEPHANIAH 3:16–17 MSG

My friend Marianne is going blind. A legitimate source of stress and even despair, wouldn't you agree?

Yet Marianne's attitude is anything but frantic. In her calm, steady voice, she explains, "When I start to worry or obsess, I recite the facts I know to be true":

- *"God is in control."*
- *"He loves me."*
- *"He wants what's best for me, even though my ideas may not be His."*
- *"I will only find peace by resting in His will. Fighting, kicking, and screaming will only lead to a miserable, wasted life."*

*Dear Papa God, it's difficult not to despair in
a horrible situation. Please remind me of all
that is true about Your goodness and love,
and help me to trust You more. Amen.*

GLAD TO BE WEAK

Three times I begged the Lord to make this suffering go away. But he replied, "My kindness is all you need. My power is strongest when you are weak."
2 CORINTHIANS 12:8–9 CEV

Because of her failing vision, my friend Marianne lost her job and the ability to do many of the things she loved. She has every right to be angry. Resentful. Bitter. But amazingly, she's not.

"When I could see, I was a control person. I did what I wanted when I wanted. My prayers consisted mostly of 'Lord, please bless these plans that I've made.' But God didn't say, 'Follow Me when things are great and you have all your faculties.' He said, 'Follow Me even when you're at your worst.' That's when we learn to truly depend on Him for our every need."

Marianne smiles, her liquid brown eyes shining. "I'm not bitter; I'm better. God allowed my blindness in order to grow me. Sure, I get frustrated sometimes and wish I could see, but I wouldn't trade eyesight for this precious peace I have."

. . . .

Dear Papa God, no matter what trials come my way, please help me remember that every weakness requires me to depend on You even more. Amen.

TRUST IN GOD'S SOVEREIGNTY

We know that God is always at work for the good of everyone who loves him.
Romans 8:28 cev

Peace in the midst of life's chaos. Peace, that jumping-off platform for inexplicable joy. Peace, that elusive, anxiety-free place of freedom we long for.

I've been thinking a lot about peace lately. Why is it so hard to grasp? And when we finally do, why does it slip-slide away so quickly?

I've learned that real, honest-to-goodness peace is entirely dependent on our trust in God's sovereignty. That means believing He's in control of all the details of our lives, even if it doesn't feel like it. Only when our trust is anchored in Him can we find peace. There's nothing random or accidental about it. Trust is a decision we make. A volitional, intentional act.

* *

Dear Papa God, when my feelings are stealing my peace, please remind me of Your sovereignty. I choose to trust in You. Amen.

PEACE AMID THE TURMOIL

Naomi said, "Where did you work today? Whose field was it? God bless the man who treated you so well!" Then Ruth told her that she had worked in the field of a man named Boaz.

RUTH 2:19 CEV

Trust is the cornerstone to acquiring peace. We can relax in complete security, knowing our Creator is looking out for our best interests.

But when we slide back into the dark, slimy mudhole of thinking we are responsible for making things happen in our lives, anxiety and fear take over.

The Old Testament book of Ruth is a wonderful example of God's sovereignty in the life of a gal like you and me. A sister immersed in heartache, loneliness, and financial problems. Yet she found peace amid the turmoil.

Take ten minutes to read Ruth 2 (or better yet, the whole book—it's very short), and notice how all the random things that "just happened" to occur weren't really random at all. They were all part of God's sovereign design for Ruth.

· ·

Dear Papa God, please let Ruth's story encourage me to trust in You more. You are sovereign, and Your plans and timing are perfect. Thank You! Amen.

DAWN ALWAYS BREAKS

*Don't worry about anything, but pray about everything.
With thankful hearts offer up your prayers and
requests to God. Then, because you belong to Christ
Jesus, God will bless you with peace that no one
can completely understand. And this peace will
control the way you think and feel.*
PHILIPPIANS 4:6–7 CEV

We go through turbulent seasons, but we have to remember that the storms won't last forever. Dawn always breaks after a long, dark night. "Weeping may stay for the night, but rejoicing comes in the morning" (Psalm 30:5 NIV).

I find it seriously comforting to know God is just as sovereign today as He was in Ruth's day. He's in control of each and every detail of our lives. And the peace of God, which surpasses all human understanding, will keep our hearts and our minds out of the anxiety stress-pool.

. . . .

*Dear Papa God, You are sovereign, You never
change, and You care about every detail of my
life. Please help me to repeat these truths as
needed to keep me in Your peace. Amen.*

WHEN THE ENEMY ATTACKS

For the word of God is alive and powerful.
It is sharper than the sharpest two-edged sword.
HEBREWS 4:12 NLT

The enemy attacks when we're most vulnerable: times of fatigue, illness, or disappointment. He ravages our emotions through heartbreak, resentment, and hatred. He sours our relationships and rips our guts out to weaken us (think Braveheart here). He even exploits our secret thoughts, milking them to churn up gossip, slander, criticism.

We don't have to just duck his onslaught! We're mighty warriors! We can fight back with the only undefeatable weapon in existence—the Word of God, sharper than any two-edged sword. We must keep our arsenals full of ammo by studying our Bibles and memorizing verses so our flaming arrows are lit and ready to shoot the moment we're jumped by the enemy.

. . . .

Dear Papa God, please arm me with Your Word.
Help me to be ready for any spiritual battle. Amen.

WHOLE AND HOLY BY HIS LOVE

Long before he laid down earth's foundations,
he had us in mind, had settled on us as the focus
of his love, to be made whole and holy by his love.

EPHESIANS 1:4 MSG

Did you catch that? God's love for us isn't dependent on anything we do or don't do, blab, or omit. Our Father's love itself is what makes us whole and holy; not anything we can contrive, create, or earn. And He's had us—you and me—in mind to be the focus of His love even before the creation of our world.

What a calming, reassuring thought. Such indescribable security. To know that we are truly loved, regardless of how many times we blow it. Even if we react poorly, there's a way out. We are treasured. Cherished. Adored. Papa God wants nothing more than to cuddle with us, crooning His comfort and peace into our troubled hearts. Anytime. Anywhere. He never gives up on us, never loses hope in us, and His love endures through every circumstance.

. . . .

Dear Papa God, I am overwhelmed that You
love me so much, so unconditionally. Your love
is what carries me, and I am so grateful. Amen.

165

RELATIONSHIP, NOT RELIGION

We worship you, Lord, and we should always pray whenever we find out that we have sinned. Then we won't be swept away by a raging flood. You are my hiding place! You protect me from trouble, and you put songs in my heart because you have saved me.

PSALM 32:6–7 CEV

I don't want to approach prayer as a chore. I'm not reporting for duty or giving God instructions on what's best for me. Nor do I want my prayer life to consist merely of rhino-in-the-road desperation pleas to NeedGodNOW.com.

Above all, I don't want to get caught up in religion and miss the relationship. To get so busy learning about Him and doing a gazillion things that I call serving Him that I neglect to get to know Him. That's when Christianity becomes "nice-ianity" and all about behavior—rights and wrongs—rather than about a dynamic, daily communication with a living, loving Savior.

No, I come with a humble heart, an open mind, and a thirsty spirit. I cherish spending time with Him.

. . . .

Dear Papa God, I want to cherish my time with You! Please help me to make my relationship with You my top and favorite priority. Amen.

A HEALING SPRING OF WATER

You are my God. I worship you. In my heart,
I long for you, as I would long for a
stream in a scorching desert.

PSALM 63:1 CEV

Sometimes when we feel least like doing something, it's the very thing we need to do most. In my depression, I kept reading every day out of sheer obedience and progressed to the help-me-trust-again Psalm verses, such as "The LORD is my shepherd, I shall not want. . . . Your rod and Your staff, they comfort me" (23:1, 4 NASB); "Weeping may last for the night, but a shout of joy comes in the morning" (30:5 NASB); "I sought the LORD, and He answered me, and delivered me from all my fears" (34:4 NASB); and "Cease striving and know that I am God" (46:10 NASB). Other psalms offering hope and healing are 56, 63, 119, 121, and 139.

Within those pages I'd stumbled upon a map, but I didn't realize I was actually clawing my way out of my lost, dark cavern until I saw light peeking over the rim. God's Word seeped into my parched spirit like a healing spring of water.

• •

Dear Papa God, Your Word is a light and guide
for my path in life and a healing spring of water
when I'm dry and wounded. Thank You! Amen.

WORSHIP WHEREVER YOU ARE

"Yet a time is coming and has now come when the true worshipers will worship the Father in the Spirit and in truth, for they are the kind of worshipers the Father seeks."

JOHN 4:23 NIV

Worship doesn't have to be just in a stained glass building or magnificent cathedral or at a designated hour and location. The true church isn't an edifice; it's the people, the worshippers inside. It's us, you and me. "The real believers are the ones the Spirit of God leads to work away at this ministry, filling the air with Christ's praise as we do it" (Philippians 3:3 MSG).

Yep, we spontaneous worshippers, the ones who burst forth with unbridled praise springing from a joyful spirit, are just the kind of worshippers the Father is looking for.

. . . .

Dear Papa God, You are so worthy of my worship, the only One who is! I want to praise You wherever I am and in everything I do! Amen.

A LIFESTYLE OF TRUST

Trust in the LORD with all your heart and lean not on your own understanding; in all your ways submit to him, and he will make your paths straight.
PROVERBS 3:5–6 NIV

Trust in our heavenly Father is meant to literally become part of us. A lifestyle. A belief system woven into the fabric of our being as much as the color of our eyes.

A good example is Peter in the Garden of Gethsemane, who panicked when Judas brought soldiers to arrest Jesus. Peter hadn't yet learned to trust in the Lord with all his heart and not lean on his own understanding (see Proverbs 3:5), so he reacted in his typical, impulsive, Deb Coty-esque manner. He whipped out his ear-slicing sword, told three bald-faced lies, and skittered away from danger like a scared rabbit (see Luke 22:47–62). Peter was a person wanting desperately to trust his Jesus but was besieged by weakness and doubt. I so identify with his impetuous, leap-before-you-look, walk-on-water-until-you-realize-what-you're-doing personality (see Matthew 14:28–31).

* * *

Dear Papa God, when weakness and doubt make me lose my faith in You, please strengthen me again with Your Spirit and Your Word. I want to live and breathe my trust in You. Amen.

WHEN TRUST TRIUMPHS

But I trust in you, LORD; I say, "You are my God."
My times are in your hands; deliver me from the
hands of my enemies, from those who pursue me.
PSALM 31:14–15 NIV

Sometimes—thankfully—trust triumphs and we make good decisions. Like this very same Peter who later matured in his faith to the point where trust was second nature. Wherever God led, he followed. While imprisoned, he awoke from a dead sleep and, without waffling a single second, followed an angel (not your normal jail visitor!) past armed guards and right out through locked gates (see Acts 12:6–10).

I take great comfort in the fact that the "before" Peter could victoriously morph into the "after" Peter. If Peter could learn trust, so can I. Just because I sank in one trust plunge doesn't mean I can't bob to the surface on the next. Or the third. Or the eighty-fifth.

* *

Dear Papa God, forgive me when I fail to trust
in You, and thank You so much that You never
stop giving me chances to trust again. Amen.

LIKE A SECOND SKIN

Those who know your name trust
in you, for you, LORD, have never
forsaken those who seek you.

PSALM 9:10 NIV

Trust: such an intimate form of faith. In its purest form, we shouldn't have to remember to apply it in a crisis situation—it should kick in automatically if we truly trust the Lord with all our heart and live what we believe. Trust should cling to us like a second skin. We always have it on and don't have to think about it. It grows with us, and we can completely depend on its protection.

Thankfully, Papa God knows that it's a learning process for all of us. He's patiently waiting for our level of reliance to catch up and override our not-so-common sense as we take the plunge into trust.

. . . .

Dear Papa God, thank You for fully understanding
our learning process of trust. I'm so grateful for
Your amazing patience and love for me. Amen.

A GLORIOUS BEGINNING

"Where, O death, is your victory?
Where, O death, is your sting?"
1 CORINTHIANS 15:55 NIV

Eternal life is the dessert on the smorgasbord of faith. Walking hand in hand with our heavenly Father during our limited days on earth is marvelous enough, but the promise of being in His presence forever in heaven is almost beyond comprehension.

Pleasure and joy greater than we have ever known. Peace beyond compare. No sorrows, tears, or pain. Who wouldn't want such a glorious beginning to look forward to when our time on earth is at an end?

Dear sister, if you haven't yet taken the step of accepting Jesus Christ as your Lord and Savior, please consider doing so now. It's the most important decision you'll ever make.

. . . .

Dear Papa God, I can't even wrap my mind around
all that must be in store in the perfect home of
heaven You have waiting for us. Thank You for saving
me and for giving such a glorious beginning to look
forward to after death—eternal life with You. Amen.

ABC

Out of sheer generosity he put us in right standing with himself. A pure gift. He got us out of the mess we're in and restored us to where he always wanted us to be. And he did it by means of Jesus Christ.
ROMANS 3:23–24 MSG

Reserve your spot in heaven and begin your incredible journey of faith right this very minute. It's as simple as *ABC*.

- A: *Admitting that we need cleansed of our sins.*
- B: *Believing that Jesus died for our sins and rose from the grave.*
- C: *Committing our lives to Him is not about religion but relationship. "If you confess with your mouth Jesus as Lord, and believe in your heart that God raised Him from the dead, you will be saved" (Romans 10:9 NASB).*

Dear Papa God, please come into my life, which I commit to You. Help me to grow in my relationship with You, through Your Spirit and Your Word. Amen.

TRUST THE FATHER

So you have not received a spirit that makes you fearful slaves. Instead, you received God's Spirit when he adopted you as his own children. Now we call him, "Abba, Father."

ROMANS 8:15 NLT

When I was a little girl, my family would pile into our Plymouth station wagon for the long Thanksgiving drive to my grandmother's house in northern Georgia. My sister and I sat in the backseat, laughing, singing, and enjoying the journey, with full confidence that Daddy would drive us safely to our destination.

We didn't worry. We didn't fret. We never feared the what-ifs: What if a tire pops? What if somebody broadsides us? What if a cyclone swoops down and turns our car into a gigantic Frisbee?

We had peace because we trusted our father and knew we were safe in his hands. In the same way, Papa God is our heavenly Father and we can trust that He will get us safely where we need to be. We don't need to worry, fret, or fear the what-ifs.

. . . .

Dear Papa God, You are just that—my heavenly Papa. So much more than even a loving and kind earthly dad, You are always caring for me, protecting me, and doing what is best for me. I need never worry. Amen.

THE WHAT-IFS

Don't worry and ask yourselves, "Will we have anything to eat? Will we have anything to drink? Will we have any clothes to wear?" Only people who don't know God are always worrying about such things. Your Father in heaven knows that you need all of these.
MATTHEW 6:31–32 CEV

As grown women, we often find the what-ifs stealing our peace and adding to our emotional turmoil: What if I lose my job? What if someone finds out my secret? What if the group of women I want to be part of doesn't accept me? What if I'm not good enough? What if my children grow up to be serial killers because I was such a horrible mother?

We must remind ourselves that the what-ifs aren't real. That's Satan sticking his dirty, rotten fingers into our hearts and minds to steal the peace Papa God promises if we depend on Him as our *Abba* (intimate Hebrew form of "father"). Remember, we can't control our circumstances, but we can control our responses to those circumstances.

. . . .

Dear Papa God, it does me no good to worry about tomorrow, and Your Word commands me not to. It's so hard though! Please help me to focus on Your perfect peace and provision in all things. Amen.

JUST LIKE JOB

There was a man in the land of Uz whose name was Job; and that man was blameless, upright, fearing God and turning away from evil.

JOB 1:1 NASB

Job lost his ten children and all his earthly possessions and was covered with festering, oozing boils from head to toe. All he had left was his bitter wife. Mrs. Job lost sight of all God had done and focused only on what He didn't do. Despite the fact that she urged her husband, "Curse God and die!" (Job 2:9 NASB), Job didn't.

His response? "I *know* that my Redeemer lives" (Job 19:25 NASB, emphasis added).

· ·

Dear Papa God, the account of Job amazes and humbles me. Could I respond like he did to such horror and hardship? Please help me to have such faith in You, that no matter what I must suffer in this life I never stop praising You, certain that You are my Redeemer who lives and cares for me. Amen.

JUST LIKE JOSEPH

*Yes, I am your brother Joseph, the one you
sold into Egypt. Don't worry or blame
yourselves for what you did. God is the one
who sent me ahead of you to save lives.*

GENESIS 45:4–5 CEV

As a child, Joseph was betrayed by his jealous brothers
and sold as a slave in a foreign land. He chose to
follow God even though everything appeared to be
going wrong. He worked for years to earn his master's
trust and become head slave in the household. Then
Joe's master's lusty wife falsely accused him of
attempted rape. Joe ended up in prison for two long
years, where he worked his way up to head prisoner,
only to be forgotten and left to languish by the palace
employee he'd helped get out of prison.

But Joseph clung to his belief that God had a plan
for his life. And what a marvelous surprise ending he
had in store! (Read Genesis 45.)

- -

*Dear Papa God, Joseph had every reason
to be outraged and let bitterness consume
him, but he chose instead to keep following You
and trusting You. Help me to be like Joseph,
patiently waiting on Your perfect plans. Amen.*

177

JUST LIKE HANNAH

*Hannah prayed silently to
the LORD for a long time.*
1 SAMUEL 1:12 CEV

Hannah not only had to share her husband with another woman, but she was also barren—a public disgrace in her day. For many years, she endured the taunting of "the other woman," which caused her constant tears and, no doubt, depression. But she kept on praying until God mercifully blessed her with her heart's desire, a baby boy. Hannah's child grew up to become the mighty prophet Samuel (see 1 Samuel 1).

. . . .

*Dear Papa God, while I wait, please help me to
be like Hannah and not lose faith in my prayers
to You. Even when Your answer is not immediate,
it never means You're not listening. I know You
hear me, and I trust You to deliver and bless
exactly when You know is best. Amen.*

IN BODY AND IN SPIRIT

*The Lord has promised that he
will not leave us or desert us.*
HEBREWS 13:5 CEV

Jesus is not just our Messiah, Prince of Peace, and Savior; He's also our role model as a human facing real, heart-slamming adversity, our "God in a bod."

Right after Jesus assured His followers that, although His death was imminent, He wouldn't desert them but would always be with them through the comfort and guidance of the Holy Spirit, He gave the best parting gift ever: "I am leaving you with a gift—peace of mind and heart. And the peace I give is a gift the world cannot give. So don't be troubled or afraid" (John 14:27 NLT).

. . . .

*Dear Papa God, thank You for coming to be
our human role model. I wish I could have walked
with You in person, and sometimes I wish so
desperately that You with Your physical body were
here to guide and comfort me now. But Your Spirit
is here, and I am so grateful for that gift and
Your constant presence in my life. Amen.*

PEACE

I lift up my eyes to the mountains—where does my help come from? My help comes from the LORD, *the Maker of heaven and earth.*

PSALM 121:1–2 NIV

May I share my PEACE acronym with you? It's easy to remember and oh so helpful when your hands are feverishly gripping those last few hairs on your head and getting ready to yank.

P: *Placing*
E: *Each*
A: *Aggravation at*
C: *Christ's feet. . .*
E: *Expectantly!*

If we don't look up for Papa God's help, if we keep our eyes trained downward on our circumstances, we will eventually fall into hopelessness and despair. We'll lose our sense of purpose and no longer see hope on the horizon. "Where there is no vision, the people perish" (Proverbs 29:18 KJV).

. . . .

Dear Papa God, please help me to keep my eyes lifted up to You, not focusing on my troubles, but focusing on Your power to come to my rescue. Amen.

180

HE WILL FIND YOU

Our LORD, we belong to you. We tell you what worries us, and you won't let us fall.

PSALM 55:22 CEV

Like the parable Jesus told about the lost sheep (meaning us!) in the fifteenth chapter of Luke (read verses 1–6 to refresh your memory), we can never stray from our Shepherd to the point of no return. He loves us far too much to let us go. I find that marvelously reassuring, don't you?

So when you lose your way and begin to wander, whether it's spiritually, emotionally, mentally, or physically (hey, I can get lost in a tote bag), be assured that Papa will find you. Know why? Because you, sister, are too loved to be lost.

. . . .

Dear Papa God, I want to hold Your hand through every walk of life. Thank You for never letting go of me. Amen.

SOFTENING HEARTS OF STONE

"I will give you a new heart and put a new spirit within you; I will take the heart of stone out of your flesh and give you a heart of flesh."
EZEKIEL 36:26 NKJV

My friend Sheila works twelve-hour shifts and takes care of her mother, who suffers with dementia, and her ninety-two-year-old stepfather. Some days the stress and fatigue seem overwhelming, and Sheila feels resentful about having to forfeit her days off to do their grocery shopping, cooking, house cleaning, and laundry.

On one such day, when Sheila entered the house and began unpacking groceries, Sheila's mom wandered into the kitchen and began crying. Through warm, grateful tears, Sheila's mother thanked the Lord aloud for her daughter, for the groceries she brought, and for all she did for them.

As Sheila recalls, "My selfish attitude flew right out the window." Sheila realized that Papa God had seen her granite-hard heart prior to her arrival and knew she needed a heart transplant.

. . . .

Dear Papa God, when I'm exhausted and burned out, please refresh my spirit and soften my heart as only You can. Amen.

WELL-DESERVED GRATITUDE

Am I now trying to win the approval of human beings, or of God? Or am I trying to please people? If I were still trying to please people, I would not be a servant of Christ.

GALATIANS 1:10 NIV

You may not ever receive sufficient thanks from others for all you do, but when you feel bummed over it, remind yourself that Papa God sees every little detail and is well aware of the sacrifices and effort you make to serve others in your family, job, church, community. . . the inhabitants of your little world. Papa sees it all— every dollar you spend, all the time and energy you put in, each hour of sleep you miss—and He truly appreciates you acting as His fingers and toes on the earth.

One day He'll reward you with the immense gratitude you deserve, but brace yourself, it may not be until heaven. In the meantime, lean not on fallible people but on Papa as your source of validation and satisfaction for a job well done and a life well lived.

. . . .

Dear Papa God, help me to remember that if I'm working just to please people, I will never feel fully appreciated. But everything I do for You is seen and rewarded, if not here in this world, then in heaven for eternity. Amen.

IT IS WELL

*Praise the L*ORD*, my soul; all my inmost being,
praise his holy name. Praise the L*ORD*, my soul,
and forget not all his benefits.*

PSALM 103:1–2 NIV

Somehow, after losing nearly everything he once held dear, through Papa God's supernatural strength, Horatio Spafford was able to pen these incredible words:

*When peace like a river attendeth my way,
When sorrows like sea billows roll;
Whatever my lot, Thou hast taught me to say,
It is well, it is well with my soul.*

Wow. Snowball upside my head. Does the concept that we can attain wellness regardless of our circumstances wallop you as hard as it does me? Yet that's what almighty Yahweh can do for us. Wholeness when we're in pieces. Stability when we're fragmented. Restoration when we're broken.

· ·

*Dear Papa God, whatever my lot,
it is well with my soul. I want to be
able to say that sincerely too. Amen.*

THE THIRST OF THE SOUL

Jesus replied, "Anyone who drinks this water will soon become thirsty again. But those who drink the water I give will never be thirsty again. It becomes a fresh, bubbling spring within them, giving them eternal life."

John 4:13–14 NLT

My friend Tricia had all kinds of friends in high places. She was rich, beautiful, and famous. People adored her.

But it just wasn't enough.

Spiritually, she experienced a religious smorgasbord, dabbling in Catholicism, Protestantism, Mormonism, Buddhism, Hinduism, astral projection, and various New Age pursuits.

But despite all her effort, Tricia found herself in her early forties unsettled, unfulfilled, and unhappy. Divorced and jaded, she had found nothing that could quench the deep, racking thirst within her for love. Real love. Forever love.

Then she met Jesus.

Tricia was blown away by pure, authentic love. And once Tricia devoted herself to the Lover of her soul, His incredible love permeated every area of her life, her parched heart, and her thirsty soul.

* *

Dear Papa God, remind me that only You satisfy every desire of my soul. Amen.

YOUR LEGACY

We will not conceal them from their children,
but tell to the generation to come the
praises of the LORD, and His strength and
His wondrous works that He has done.

PSALM 78:4 NASB

What will your legacy be?

Will they remember a woman of beauty and grace, regardless of her sometimes haggard appearance? Or will that ugly, out-of-control inner beast be what they recall most?

Will it be a preoccupied wife, mother, or friend always rushing off somewhere to accomplish never-ending tasks? A woman whose priorities were so skewed that she failed to put people before things? A frantic soul who missed out on living because she chose to wrestle life instead?

Or will it be her prayer life, unconditional love, and faith that floats even in the stress-pool of life? Will it be memories of a life well lived, moments savored, laughter shared? I hope and pray that's what my legacy will be.

· ·

Dear Papa God, I'm not perfect and never will be,
but with Your help I can leave a legacy of pointing
others to You with a life full of Your love, joy,
peace, patience, kindness, goodness, faithfulness,
gentleness, and self-control. Amen.

SCRIPTURE INDEX

ABOUT THE AUTHOR

Debora M. Coty is a popular speaker, columnist, lifelong Bible student, and award-winning author of numerous books, including the bestselling *Too Blessed to be Stressed* series. She's also a piano teacher, retired occupational therapist, and tennis addict. Deb lives, loves, and laughs in central Florida with her husband of forty years, just down the road from her two grown children and four audacious grands. Visit with Deb online at www.DeboraCoty.com.